EDITOR: Maryanne Blacker

FOOD EDITOR: Pamela Clark

■ ■ ■

DESIGNER: Robbylee Phelan

■ ■ ■

HOME ECONOMISTS: Barbara Northwood, Laura Robertson, Lucy Clayton, Wendy Berecry, Michelle Gorry

■ ■ ■

DEPUTY FOOD EDITOR: Jan Castorina

ASSISTANT FOOD EDITOR: Kathy Snowball

ASSOCIATE FOOD EDITOR: Enid Morrison

EDITORIAL COORDINATOR: Elizabeth Hooper

KITCHEN ASSISTANT: Amy Wong

■ ■ ■

STYLIST: Jacqui Hing

PHOTOGRAPHERS: Russell Brooks, Luis Martin, Kent Mears, Warwick Kent, Andrew Payne, Patrick Byrne

■ ■ ■

HOME LIBRARY STAFF:

ASSISTANT EDITOR: Beverley Hudec

ART DIRECTOR Paula Wooller

EDITORIAL COORDINATOR: Fiona Nicholas

■ ■ ■

ACP PUBLISHER: Richard Walsh

ACP DEPUTY PUBLISHER: Nick Chan

■ ■ ■

Produced by The Australian Women's Weekly Home Library. Typeset by ACP Colour Graphics Pty Ltd. Printed by Dai Nippon Co Ltd in Japan. Published by ACP Publishing 54 Park Street Sydney.
♦ AUSTRALIA: Distributed by Network Distribution Company, 54 Park Street Sydney, (02) 282 8777.
♦ UNITED KINGDOM: Distributed in the U.K. by ACP Publishing (UK) Ltd , 20 Galowhill Rd, Brackmills, Northampton NN4 OOE, (0604) 760 456.
♦ NEW ZEALAND: Distributed in New Zealand by Netlink Distribution Company, 17B Hargreaves St, Level 5, College Hill, Auckland 1, (9) 302 7616.
♦ CANADA: Distributed in Canada by Whitecap Books Ltd, 1086 West 3rd St, North Vancouver V7P 3J6, (604) 9809852.
♦ SOUTH AFRICA: Distributed in South Africa by Intermag, PO Box 57394, Springfield 2137, (011) 4933200.
ACN 053 273 546

■ ■ ■

Easy Entertaining.
Includes index
ISBN 0 949128 40 6.

1. Cookery. 2. Entertaining. 1. Australian Women's Weekly.

641.5

■ ■ ■

■ ■ ■

FRONT COVER: : Fresh Watercress Soup, Rack of Lamb with Tasty Vegetable Sauce from the Low Joule Dinner Party for Four, page 31.
China from Villeroy & Boch.
BACK COVER: Strawberry Mousse Hazelnut Torte from the Wedding Breakfast for 50, page 71.
China from Villeroy & Boch.
OPPOSITE: Prawn and Oyster Platter with Cocktail Sauce and Chive Mayonnaise from the Australian Dinner Party for 10, page 52.
INSIDE BACK COVER: Antipasto Platter from the Italian-Style Dinner Party for 10, page 12.

Entertaining at home is increasingly popular. In this collection of about 200 recipes, there is something for every occasion and age group. We tell you how far ahead each recipe can be made, if you can freeze and/or microwave individual recipes and how to do it. Emphasis is on easy cooking but where needed we have included step-by-step instructions. As usual, all our recipes are pictured.

Pamela Clark
FOOD EDITOR

D0534133

BRITISH & NORTH AMERICAN READERS: Please note that Australian cup and spoon measurements are metric. A quick conversion guide appears on page 128.
A glossary explaining unfamiliar terms and ingredients appears on page 125.

Menus for all Occasions

Useful Information

MICROWAVE

It is important you read the instruction manual that accompanies your oven.

Domestic microwave ovens at present on the market vary in watt output, roughly between 500 and 700 watts. All the recipes in this book were tested on a 600-watt oven. If your oven has a higher or lower output than 600 watts, add or deduct a little cooking time to the recipe.

The oven we used had quite a lot of settings. We have tried to use HIGH in most recipes in this book — presuming everyone is in a hurry. However, the MEDIUM is about 70 percent power, MEDIUM HIGH 90 percent and MEDIUM LOW 50 percent power. If your oven has HIGH and DEFROST only you will have to start on HIGH and go back to DEFROST to continue cooking.

Times given in our recipes are only for your guidance. Always check food after minimum suggested cooking time.

EQUIPMENT TO USE

If in doubt about the suitability of a dish or plate, etc., for use in a microwave oven, stand the dish in the oven with a glass of water next to it. Turn the control to HIGH, set for a minute. If the dish remains cold, it is fine for use, if (like the water) it gets hot do not use it in the microwave oven.

Food will cook more evenly and faster in a shallow, straight-sided round or oval dish rather than in a deeper dish of the same capacity.

Do not use dishes with metal rim or handles, etc., fine crystal or Melamine® or Centura® bowls or plates.

Styrofoam®, plastic storage and icecream containers can be used for reheating some food as long as the food is not too high in butter, oil, sugar or honey content. The food, when hot, will distort the plastic. Do not use these containers to cook raw food.

Foil food trays can be used if they are at least two thirds full. Keep trays about 2.5cm away from walls and door of oven.

We used plastic food wrap to cover foods when necessary; allow a little vent for steam to escape. Be careful of steam when removing food wrap — do this away from you. Cover food in the microwave oven, if you would cover it when cooked conventionally or if you want to retain moisture. Always cover food when reheating.

COOKING TIMES

The golden rule is to UNDERCOOK all food, check to see if it is done to your liking and return it to the oven if necessary. Remember, 30 seconds or less can mean the difference between food being properly cooked or not.

EXTRA TIPS

Use your microwave for:
- Heating well wrung out hand towels on HIGH 1 minute.
- Melting chocolate, butter, jam, honey, liquid glucose, etc.
- Softening cream cheese and butter.
- Individual serves of coffee, mulled wine, soups, hot chocolate, Irish Coffee, etc.
- To heat plates, layer up to 6 plates with a well wrung out sheet of absorbent paper between each. Microwave on HIGH for 2 minutes. Do not use plates with silver or gold trim in the microwave oven.

FREEZING

When freezing food it is important that the food be fresh and, if baked, that it is cooled rapidly, then frozen as quickly as possible. If freezing a vegetable or meat casserole type of recipe, it is a good idea to stand the dish in iced water to drop the temperature of the food as fast as possible, then seal airtight and freeze. There are several different methods of freezing food. If using screw or clip-top lids, always leave about 2.5cm of headspace between the surface of the food and the top of the lid, this allows room for the food to expand during freezing. If using freezer wrap or bags, make sure as much air as possible is excluded for best results. Foil can be used; once again, wrap tightly to exclude air. Foil is particularly useful for foods such as bread, muffins, etc., which need to be returned to the oven to thaw and reheat before serving.

SUGGESTED KEEPING TIMES FOR FREEZING FOODS

	Months
Bacon	1
Beef	6
Chicken	6
Cakes	2
Cooked casseroles	2
Cooked soups	2
Crab	3
Fish	3
Ham	1
Lamb	6
Lobster	3
Pork	4
Prawns	3
Turkey	6
Veal	6

A little more time and effort are required for this dinner party. Boning out quail is easy once you begin, and it's well worth the trouble for appearance and easy eating.

AN ELEGANT DINNER PARTY FOR SIX

SEAFOOD TARTLETS WITH LEMON SAFFRON SAUCE
SEASONED BRANDIED QUAIL
HONEYED WILD RICE WITH SHREDDED VEGETABLES
SAUCY CHOCOLATE AND COFFEE ICECREAM

SEAFOOD TARTLETS WITH LEMON SAFFRON SAUCE

Bake pastry cases, cool to room temperature, store in single layer (they are fragile) in an airtight container for up to a week. If weather is wet or humid, store in refrigerator. Prepare seafood on day of serving, prepare sauce an hour or two before required, cover surface of sauce with plastic food wrap to prevent skin forming.

PASTRY
1¾ cups plain flour
125g butter
2 egg yolks
1 tablespoon water, approximately
SEAFOOD FILLING
30g butter
1 clove garlic, crushed
⅓ cup thickened cream
¼ teaspoon grated lemon rind
1 tablespoon lemon juice
saffron powder
200g scallops
100g squid
500g green king prawns, shelled
chives

Pastry: Sift flour into bowl, rub in butter, add egg yolks and enough water to mix to a firm dough. Turn pastry onto lightly floured surface, knead lightly. Divide pastry into 6; shape pieces into rounds, wrap individually in plastic food wrap, refrigerate 20 minutes. Roll pieces of pastry on lightly floured surface to rounds large enough to line 6 x 10cm flan tins, trim edges, prick bases all over with fork. Bake in moderately hot oven 10 to 15 minutes or until pastry is light golden brown; cool, remove from tins. Place cold pastry cases on oven tray, reheat in moderate oven 5 minutes. Place on warm serving plates, fill with Seafood Filling. Serve immediately, garnished with chives.

Seafood Filling: Melt butter in pan with garlic, cook 1 minute, add cream, lemon rind and juice, simmer uncovered 3 minutes; add tiny pinch of saffron powder (just enough to color the sauce a light lemon yellow). Clean scallops, separate coral, leave scallops whole. Clean squid, cut tubes open, score the inside in a diamond pattern, cut into 3cm pieces. Devein prawns, cut in half. Add seafood to sauce, simmer 2 minutes or until heated through.
Note: This recipe is not suitable to freeze or microwave.

Dinner service is Wedgwood Colonnade; glasses are Mikasa Sea Mist.

HONEYED WILD RICE WITH SHREDDED VEGETABLES

Wild rice can be boiled the day before and reheated by boiling with the long grain rice for 10 minutes.

1 cup wild rice
½ cup long grain rice
30g butter
2 medium carrots, grated
2 small zucchini, grated
1 tablespoon honey
2 teaspoons soy sauce

Bring large pan of water to boil, add wild rice, boil 30 minutes, drain. Bring separate large pan of water to boil, add long grain rice, boil 10 minutes or until rice is tender; drain.

Heat butter in pan, add carrots, zucchini and honey, cook stirring 2 minutes. Combine both types of rice with vegetables and soy sauce.

■ **TO MICROWAVE:** Prepare both types of rice as above. Cook carrots, zucchini and honey in butter in dish on HIGH 2 minutes, add both types of drained rice, cook on HIGH 3 minutes or until hot, add soy sauce.

Note: This recipe is not suitable to freeze.

Below: Saucy Chocolate and Coffee Icecream.

SEASONED BRANDIED QUAIL

Quail can be boned up to a week before and frozen. Season and sew quail on day of serving.

12 quail
¼ cup oil
1½ tablespoons cornflour
1½ cups chicken stock
1½ tablespoons brandy
FILLING
3 medium(500g) potatoes, chopped
5 bacon rashers, finely chopped
2 onions, finely chopped
2 cloves garlic, crushed
14 spinach leaves, shredded
130g can diced capsicum, drained

Remove ribcages from quail as shown in adjoining column. Spoon filling down centre of each quail, fold one side over, then the other. Sew flesh together using needle and thread. Tie drumsticks together with thread. Place quail in single layer in shallow baking dish, brush with oil. Bake in moderate oven 40 minutes or until tender and golden brown, brushing occasionally with oil. Remove thread, place quail onto serving plate, keep warm. Discard all but 2 tablespoons of pan drippings. Place dish on top of stove, add cornflour, stir over heat 1 minute. Add stock and brandy, stir constantly until sauce boils and thickens. Serve sauce over quail.

Filling: Boil or steam potatoes until tender, drain, mash. Saute bacon, onion and garlic in pan until onion is tender. Add spinach and capsicum, stir over heat until spinach has wilted. Drain away liquid, stir in potato.

Note: This recipe is not suitable to freeze or microwave.

TO BONE OUT RIBCAGE OF QUAIL
STEP 1
Run knife down both sides of ribcage of each quail.

STEP 2
Carefully cut away ribcage from flesh; leave wings and legs intact.

SAUCY CHOCOLATE AND COFFEE ICECREAM

The Chocolate Sauce remains soft during the freezing of this icecream. This will give it a self-saucing effect.

CHOCOLATE SAUCE
185g dark chocolate, chopped
⅓ cup water
60g butter
½ cup icing sugar
1 tablespoon brandy
COFFEE ICECREAM
3 eggs
⅔ cup castor sugar
1 tablespoon instant coffee powder
1 tablespoon hot water
2 x 300ml cartons thickened cream, whipped

Chocolate Sauce: Combine chocolate, water and butter in pan, stir over low heat without boiling until chocolate is melted. Stir in icing sugar and brandy over heat. Pour mixture into a loaf tin, cover with foil, freeze several hours or overnight.

Coffee Icecream: Combine eggs and sugar in pan, whisk constantly over low heat without boiling until frothy and slightly thickened. Dissolve coffee in water, add to egg mixture, cool to room temperature. Fold cream into coffee mixture. Pour into loaf tin, cover with foil, freeze until almost set. Remove Coffee Icecream, beat with wooden spoon until soft. Place some Coffee Icecream over base of loaf tin, then top with alternate spoonfuls of Coffee Icecream and frozen Chocolate Sauce until both mixtures have been used. Freeze overnight covered with foil.

■ **TO FREEZE:** This icecream can be made and frozen, covered, for up to 2 weeks ahead, if desired.

FINISHING TOUCHES

TOFFEE DIPPED FRUITS

Choose firm, unblemished fruits. We used grapes and strawberries; they support toffee better than softer fruits such as mandarin segments. You will need to make a small quantity of toffee an hour or two before you are ready to serve the fruit. If you want to dip a lot of fruit it is easier to do it in several small batches rather than try to keep the toffee runny enough for a long time.

Place 1 cup of white sugar into a medium sized heavy based pan, add ½ cup water. Stir constantly over a fairly high heat without boiling until the sugar is dissolved. This is important. If the sugar grains are still visible when the syrup boils, it will crystallise, and you will have to start again. Once the sugar is dissolved, bring to the boil without stirring and boil rapidly uncovered until the syrup turns the color of honey. Remove it from the heat and drop a teaspoon of the syrup into a cup of cold water; it will set immediately and snap between your fingers if it is ready. If not, it will still be runny, in which case, cook the syrup longer.

Have the fruit ready to dip. Use a skewer to support the grapes by the stems, pierce the strawberries near the stem to dip the berries. If you are careful, hold the fruit by the stem to toffee dip. Hold the fruit over the toffee to drain away excess toffee, then set the fruit on foil or parchment paper. They are ready to eat almost immediately, but will stand at room temperature for an hour or two. Use the fruit as a decoration on a cake or dessert, or to serve after dinner with coffee.

CHOCOLATE CURLS

Heat chopped chocolate over hot water, spread onto marble slab or laminated surface. Leave chocolate to set at room temperature, if possible. Do not let it set too hard or it will flake. Draw a long sharp knife at a slight angle across the surface of the chocolate, using a light sawing action. Allow the chocolate curls to become firm before handling.

The dark cooking compound chocolate is not suitable for making curls.

This is a deliciously different combination of flavors, sure to impress your dinner guests.

DELICIOUS DINNER PARTY FOR SIX

CHICKEN AND PINENUT-STUFFED TOMATOES

SPINACH FISH ROLLS WITH DILL BUTTER SAUCE

PUMPKIN STICKS WITH BACON AND CUMIN

POTATO, AVOCADO AND ONION BAKE

MINT BAVAROIS WITH WARM CHOCOLATE SAUCE

CHICKEN AND PINENUT-STUFFED TOMATOES

Prepare tomatoes up to 12 hours before serving, if desired.

1 cup cooked finely chopped chicken
6 medium firm ripe tomatoes
2 tablespoons pinenuts
2 tablespoons mayonnaise
2 tablespoons chopped chives
15g butter
1 onion, finely chopped
1 clove garlic, crushed
1 tablespoon sultanas

Cut tops neatly off tomatoes. Carefully scoop out pulp, puree pulp in blender or processor, strain. Stir in mayonnaise and 1 tablespoon of the chives. Toast pinenuts on oven tray in moderate oven for 5 minutes.

Heat butter in pan, add onion, saute until transparent, add garlic, saute further 1 minute, combine with pinenuts, chicken, sultanas, remaining chives and half the tomato puree. Fill tomatoes with chicken mixture. Place lids on top, serve with remaining tomato puree as a sauce.
Note: This recipe is not suitable to freeze or microwave.

POTATO, AVOCADO AND ONION BAKE

1kg new potatoes
30g butter
1 large onion, sliced
1 large avocado, chopped

Cut unpeeled potatoes into 3cm chunks, place onto oven tray, bake in moderate oven 30 minutes, turn potatoes, bake further 20 minutes. Place into ovenproof dish. Heat butter in pan, add onion, cook, stirring until soft, sprinkle over potatoes with avocado. Bake in moderate oven further 10 minutes or until heated through.
Note: This recipe is not suitable to freeze or microwave.

Dinner service is Wedgwood Touraine.

SPINACH FISH ROLLS WITH DILL BUTTER SAUCE

Prepare this dish several hours ahead of cooking time; keep covered and refrigerated until baking time. The Sauce must be made just before serving.

6 white fish fillets (e.g., bream)
250g packet frozen chopped
  spinach, thawed
15g butter
125g mushrooms, chopped
4 green shallots, chopped
1 clove garlic, crushed
1 cup stale breadcrumbs
2 tablespoons chopped parsley
60g feta cheese, crumbled
¼ cup dry white wine
DILL BUTTER SAUCE
2 tablespoons white vinegar
4 green shallots, chopped
125g unsalted butter
2 tablespoons chopped dill
  (or ½ teaspoon dried dill tips)

Skin and bone fish. Press as much liquid as possible from spinach. Heat butter in pan, add mushrooms, shallots and garlic, cook stirring for a few minutes, stir in breadcrumbs, parsley, cheese and spinach. Place spinach mixture on skin side of each fish fillet, fold over fish, secure with toothpicks. Place fish rolls in baking dish, add wine, cover, bake in moderately hot oven 12 minutes. Strain liquid from baking dish; you will need ⅓ cup liquid. Keep fish warm while making Sauce.
Dill Butter Sauce: Combine reserved ⅓ cup fish stock with vinegar and shallots, bring to boil, boil uncovered until liquid has reduced to half; strain. Melt half the butter, add to vinegar mixture. Gradually whisk in the remaining hard butter in small pieces until sauce is thick and creamy; add dill.
■ **TO MICROWAVE:** Cook filled fish rolls, covered, on HIGH 7 minutes or until fish is tender. Strain liquid. Prepare Sauce as above.
Note: This recipe is not suitable to freeze.

MINT BAVAROIS WITH WARM CHOCOLATE SAUCE

Both the Bavarois and Chocolate Sauce can be made completely the day before required; if the Bavarois is made any further in advance it will toughen. Wash and dry mint well before use.

4 egg yolks
¼ cup sugar
1 cup milk
1 bunch mint (about 1 cup leaves, firmly packed)
3 teaspoons gelatine
2 tablespoons water
300ml carton thickened cream, whipped.
CHOCOLATE SAUCE
125g dark chocolate, chopped
¼ cup water
1 tablespoon Tia Maria or Kahlua

Beat egg yolks and sugar in small bowl with electric mixer until thick and lemon colored. Heat milk, add mint leaves, remove from heat, stand 15 minutes. Blend or process milk mixture until mint is finely chopped, strain, discard mint. Add milk to egg yolk mixture, return mixture to pan, stir constantly over low heat without boiling until mixture thickens slightly. Add gelatine to water, dissolve over hot water, add to custard mixture, cool to room temperature. Combine custard mixture with cream, pour mixture into lightly oiled 1-litre mould, refrigerate overnight or several hours until set. Turn onto serving plate, serve with warm Chocolate Sauce.

Chocolate Sauce: Melt chocolate and water over low heat without boiling, add Tia Maria.

Note: This recipe is not suitable to freeze or microwave.

PUMPKIN STICKS WITH BACON AND CUMIN

Pumpkin can be cooked in the morning; refrigerate until required.

750g butternut pumpkin
30g butter
3 bacon rashers, finely chopped
½ teaspoon ground cumin

Cut pumpkin into short lengths, boil or steam until just tender, drain, place into iced water to cool, drain again.

Melt butter in pan, add bacon, cook stirring until bacon is crisp. Add cumin and pumpkin to pan, stir-fry until heated through.

■ **TO MICROWAVE:** Place pumpkin in shallow dish, add ¼ cup water, cover, cook on HIGH 6 minutes or until pumpkin is tender, drain, place into iced water, drain. Combine butter and bacon in shallow dish, cook on HIGH 4 minutes or until bacon is crisp; add cumin and pumpkin, cook on HIGH 4 minutes or until heated through.

Note: This recipe is not suitable to freeze.

MAKING A PIPING BAG

MAKING A PAPER PIPING BAG
STEP 1
Cut a 30cm square of greaseproof paper in half diagonally, to give two triangles. Place one triangle on flat surface with the apex facing you. Curl the right hand point under, bringing it toward you until it meets the apex.

STEP 2
Hold the two joined corners together with your left hand while you pick up the remaining point with your right hand. Wrap this remaining point around anti-clockwise toward you to meet the other two points which are already joined. You now have a cone.

STEP 3
Hold the cone with both hands, thumbs inside and slide the two outside points in opposite directions to draw cone tip into a tight sharp point.

STEP 4
Sticky-tape the outside seam of the cone near the top to hold it together.

STEP 5
Place bag in jug, fill with melted chocolate, fold ends of bag in to enclose chocolate.

STEP 6
Cut the tip of the cone with scissors.

Entertaining Italian-style is sure to be a winner with your friends. The food is tasty, easy to prepare and looks attractive.

ITALIAN-STYLE DINNER PARTY FOR 10

ANTIPASTO PLATTER

PASTA WITH MUSSELS AND FENNEL

CHEESY CRUMBED VEAL WITH MUSHROOM SAUCE

CRISPY BACON-TOPPED POTATOES

GARLIC BEANS

AMARETTO CHOCOLATE BOX

COFFEE NOUGAT

We suggest you serve the Antipasto Platter with drinks when your guests arrive. Then seat your guests and begin the meal with the pasta.

ANTIPASTO PLATTER

Prepare the salads a day in advance to allow flavors to develop; keep covered and refrigerated. Arrange the salads, salami and fruit on lettuce leaves just before serving. We suggest you serve at least another 500g salami and/or prosciutto with rockmelon, artichoke hearts, olives, etc.

MUSHROOM AND BLACK OLIVE SALAD

250g baby mushrooms
¾ cup (150g) black olives, pitted
1 small red pepper, chopped
6 green shallots, chopped
½ cup bottled italian dressing
Combine all ingredients in bowl. Cover, refrigerate until serving time.

CANNELLINI BEAN AND RADISH SALAD

2 x 310g cans butter beans (cannellini style)
8 radishes, thinly sliced
2 tablespoons olive oil
2 tablespoons lemon juice
1 clove garlic, crushed
¼ cup chopped parsley
Drain and rinse beans under cold water, combine in bowl with radishes. Add oil, lemon juice, garlic and parsley, toss well. Cover, refrigerate until serving time.

ZUCCHINI FENNEL MARINADE

4 medium zucchini
½ small fennel bulb
2 cloves garlic
¼ cup olive oil
2 tablespoons lemon juice
1 tablespoon finely chopped fennel leaves
Cut zucchini into matchstick lengths. Finely chop fennel, combine with zucchini in bowl. Crush garlic, add to oil, stand several hours, pour over vegetables in bowl. Toss in lemon juice and fennel leaves. Cover, refrigerate until serving time.

ANTIPASTO SPREAD

180g can chunk style tuna, drained
½ x 425g can artichoke hearts, drained
½ cup finely chopped bottled pimiento
½ cup finely chopped black olives
¼ cup chopped capers
¼ cup mayonnaise
1 clove garlic, crushed
1 teaspoon dried basil leaves
1 tablespoon lemon juice
Combine tuna, finely chopped artichoke hearts, pimiento and olives in bowl, mix well, stir in remaining ingredients. Or blend all ingredients together for a few seconds in processor. Store covered in refrigerator until serving time.

Various suggestions for an Antipasto Platter. Recipes are:
Back: Cannellini Bean and Radish Salad; Mushroom and Black Olive Salad.
Front: Antipasto Spread; Zucchini Fennel Marinade.
Tiles are Pink Esterel from Fred Pazotti; China is Spring from Studio Haus; Glasses are Susan from Orrefors and Cutlery is Boda Nova from Kosta-Boda.

PASTA WITH MUSSELS AND FENNEL

15g butter
1 onion, chopped
2 cloves garlic, crushed
2 small fennel bulbs, chopped
400g can tomatoes
2 chicken stock cubes
2 tablespoons tomato paste
4 cups water
750g mussels
¼ cup chopped parsley
½ cup cream
¼ cup grated parmesan cheese
1 kg spiral pasta

Heat butter in large pan, add onion, cook stirring until golden brown, add garlic and fennel, stir over heat 5 minutes, add undrained crushed tomatoes, crumbled stock cubes, tomato paste and water, mix well. Bring to the boil, reduce heat, simmer uncovered 45 minutes; add mussels, cook over low heat until mussels open, discard unopened shells. Add cream, parsley and parmesan cheese. Serve with pasta which has been boiled in a large pan of boiling water until just tender, drain.

Note: This recipe is not suitable to freeze or microwave.

CRISPY BACON-TOPPED POTATOES

Bacon topping can be prepared a day before required, if desired.

5 medium potatoes
oil, salt
3 bacon rashers, finely chopped
1 onion, chopped
130g can diced capsicum, drained
3 green shallots, chopped
1½ cups grated tasty cheese
2 tablespoons grated parmesan cheese
2 tablespoons chopped parsley

Pierce potato skins all over with fork, rub with oil and salt. Bake in moderate oven 1 hour.

Saute bacon and onion in pan until bacon is crisp. Add remaining ingredients, stir 1 minute. Top halved potatoes with bacon mixture, bake in moderate oven 10 minutes.

■ **TO MICROWAVE:** Place prepared potatoes around outer edge of turntable, cook on HIGH 10 minutes or until tender, stand 10 minutes. Cook bacon and onion in bowl on HIGH 4 minutes, add remaining ingredients.

Note: This recipe is not suitable to freeze.

GARLIC BEANS

1kg green beans
1 red pepper, finely chopped
2 tablespoons olive oil
1 clove garlic, crushed
1 tablespoon lemon juice

Top and tail beans, cut in half lengthwise. Bring pan of water to boil, add beans, cook 15 minutes or until just tender; drain. Combine beans, pepper, oil, garlic and lemon juice. Serve hot.

■ **TO MICROWAVE:** Cook beans in shallow dish with 1 tablespoon water, covered, on HIGH 10 minutes. Proceed as above.

Note: This recipe is not suitable to freeze.

CHEESY CRUMBED VEAL WITH MUSHROOM SAUCE

Veal can be crumbed the day before required, covered, refrigerated. Sauce can be made the day before, refrigerated and gently reheated when ready to serve.

1¼ kg veal steaks
3 onions, sliced
¼ cup dry sherry
⅓ cup brandy
plain flour
3 eggs, lightly beaten
2 cups packaged breadcrumbs
½ cup grated parmesan cheese
125g butter
MUSHROOM SAUCE
90g butter
750g baby mushrooms, halved
¼ cup plain flour
1½ cups beef stock
½ cup sour cream

Pound veal lightly with meat mallet, combine veal in shallow dish with onion, sherry and brandy for at least 4 hours, drain, reserve juice and onion for Sauce, pat meat dry. Toss meat in flour, dip in eggs, roll in combined breadcrumbs and parmesan cheese. Cook veal in about 4 batches by melting 30g of the butter in large pan, cook quarter of the veal on each side, remove, wipe pan with absorbent paper, add more butter; continue until all veal is cooked. Keep veal warm in oven. Serve with Mushroom Sauce.

Mushroom Sauce: Melt butter in pan, add reserved onions, saute until tender, add mushrooms, cook 2 minutes. Stir in flour, cook 1 minute. Stir in stock with reserved juices from veal, cook stirring until mixture boils and thickens; add sour cream.

■ **TO MICROWAVE:** Mushroom Sauce can be microwaved by combining butter and onion in shallow dish, cook on HIGH 5 minutes or until onion is tender. Add mushrooms, cook on HIGH 2 minutes. Stir in flour, then stock and reserved juice from veal, cook on HIGH 5 minutes or until mixture boils and thickens, stirring occasionally. Add sour cream. Veal is not suitable to microwave.

■ **TO FREEZE:** Veal steaks can be crumbed and frozen for up to 2 months. Thaw when required. Mushroom Sauce is not suitable to freeze.

Left: Pasta with Mussels and Fennel.
Above: Crispy Bacon-Topped Potatoes.
Below: Cheesy Crumbed Veal with Mushroom Sauce and Garlic Beans.
Cutlery is Hampton Gold by Mikasa.

AMARETTO CHOCOLATE BOX

Cake and filling can be made the day before, assembled and left covered in the refrigerator overnight. Prepare Topping up to 2 hours before serving, toffeed fruit will become sticky on standing.

ALMOND SPONGE
3 eggs
½ cup castor sugar
½ cup self-raising flour
¼ cup cornflour
¼ cup ground almonds
2 tablespoons Amaretto liqueur
¼ cup milk

CHOCOLATE AMARETTO FILLING
200g ricotta cheese
150g dark chocolate
¼ cup thickened cream
1 tablespoon Amaretto liqueur
TOPPING
2 cups sugar
1½ cups water
250g punnet strawberries
125g green grapes
125g black grapes
300ml carton thickened cream
1 tablespoon Amaretto liqueur
½ x 250g box Chocolate Coffee Thins

Almond Sponge: Beat eggs in small bowl with electric mixer until thick and creamy. Gradually add sugar, beat until sugar is dissolved. Transfer mixture to large bowl. Lightly fold in sifted flour and cornflour, then ground almonds. Pour into greased and lined deep 20cm-square cake tin; bake in moderate oven 20 minutes. Turn onto wire rack to cool. When cold, split cake in half horizontally. Brush both layers with combined Amaretto and milk. Place 1 layer of cake onto serving plate, spread with Chocolate Amaretto Filling, top with remaining layer of cake. Spread top and sides with Amaretto cream, place Chocolate Coffee Thins around sides of cake, decorate with remaining Amaretto cream and toffee dipped fruit.

Chocolate Amaretto Filling: Beat ricotta cheese in small bowl with electric mixer until smooth. Melt half the chocolate over hot water cool slightly, beat into ricotta cheese, mix in cream and Amaretto. Grate remaining chocolate, stir into ricotta cheese mixture.

Topping: Combine sugar and water in pan, stir constantly over heat until sugar is dissolved. Boil rapidly without stirring for about 15 minutes or until golden brown. Dip whole strawberries and small bunches of grapes into hot toffee, place on lightly greased tray to set. Whip cream until soft peaks form, fold in Amaretto.

■ **TO FREEZE:** Baked sponge can be wrapped and frozen for up to 2 months.

Note: This recipe is not suitable to microwave.

COFFEE NOUGAT

Glucose syrup is available from health food stores and some supermarkets. There is no substitute for this syrup.

250g blanched almonds
2 cups sugar
½ cup honey
1 cup glucose syrup
¼ cup water
2 egg whites
2 tablespoons instant coffee powder
1 tablespoon water, extra
2 teaspoons vanilla

Line base of 23cm-square slab tin with rice paper (if rice paper is not available, use a greased tin). Place almonds on oven tray, bake in moderate oven 5 minutes or until golden brown; cool. Combine sugar, honey, glucose and water in pan, stir over heat until sugar is dissolved. Boil rapidly uncovered for about 10 minutes or until mixture forms a hard ball when tested in a cup of cold water (122°C on sweets thermometer). Beat egg whites in large basin of electric mixer until stiff peaks form; pour approximately one quarter of hot syrup in thin stream over egg whites while beating constantly. Continue beating until mixture is thick enough to hold its own shape, about 3 to 5 minutes. Cook remaining syrup uncovered for about 5 minutes or until a small amount of syrup forms brittle threads when dropped in cold water ("crack" or 154°C on sweets thermometer). Pour remainder of hot syrup over meringue in a thin stream, beating constantly until mixture is very thick. Using a wooden spoon, stir in combined coffee, extra water, vanilla and toasted almonds. Spread mixture evenly into tin, place more rice paper on top, refrigerate until firm. With a sharp knife cut into pieces. It may be necessary to dip the knife into boiling water, dry it, then cut the Nougat. Store in refrigerator. Pieces may be individually wrapped in cellophane.

Makes about 50 pieces.

This is an instant dinner party which can be cooked with very little notice. The main ingredients are all fairly standard pantry or cupboard stock.

DINNER PARTY FOR SIX FROM THE PANTRY

CURRIED ASPARAGUS SOUP

PASTA WITH SALMON AND CREAM

SALAD

MOIST CHOCOLATE DESSERT CAKE

Cream and strawberries, bread and salad ingredients will have to be bought. If possible, buy fresh pasta and fresh parmesan cheese for tastiest results.

CURRIED ASPARAGUS SOUP

This soup can be prepared several hours in advance, add parsley and vermouth just before serving. We used a mild curry powder for this recipe.

1 teaspoon butter
1 onion, finely chopped
1 teaspoon curry powder
440g can cream of asparagus soup
2½ cups milk
340g can green asparagus spears, drained, chopped
1 tablespoon dry vermouth
2 tablespoons chopped parsley
Heat butter in pan, add onion and curry powder, saute until onion is tender. Stir in undiluted soup and milk, bring to boil. Stir in asparagus, return to the boil. Just before serving, stir in vermouth and parsley.
■ **TO FREEZE:** Omit parsley and vermouth. Pour cold soup into container, seal, freeze for up to 2 months. Reheat gently, or thaw overnight in refrigerator before reheating. Stir in parsley and vermouth just before serving.
■ **TO MICROWAVE:** Cook butter, onion and curry powder in bowl on HIGH 5 minutes. Add undiluted soup and milk, cook on HIGH 4 minutes or until soup reaches boiling point. Stir in asparagus, cook on HIGH 3 minutes, or until heated through. Stir in vermouth and parsley just before serving.

PASTA WITH SALMON AND CREAM

Packaged pasta will take about 10 minutes to cook, depending on type used. Freshly made pasta — quite readily available now — will take only 3 to 5 minutes to cook. We chose to use a combination of red pepper-flavored and plain fettucine. This recipe must be made and served immediately. It does not reheat successfully. We suggest you serve some fresh crusty bread and a tossed salad with this course.

750g pasta
440g can red salmon, drained
1½ x 300ml cartons cream
2 cloves garlic, crushed
2 tablespoons chopped fresh dill (or ½ teaspoon dried dill tips)
4 green shallots, chopped
2 tablespoons lemon juice
⅓ cup grated parmesan cheese
Cook pasta in large pan of boiling water until just tender, drain. Combine roughly chopped salmon in large bowl with cream, garlic, dill, shallots, lemon juice and cheese, add hot pasta, toss well, serve immediately.
Note: This recipe is not suitable to freeze or microwave.

MOIST CHOCOLATE DESSERT CAKE

Cake can be made the day before needed, cooled and kept in an airtight container.

200g dark chocolate, chopped
90g butter
5 eggs, separated
¾ cup castor sugar
⅓ cup self-raising flour, sifted
300ml carton thickened cream, whipped
250g punnet strawberries, halved
Melt chocolate and butter over hot water, remove from heat, stir in egg yolks, sugar and flour. Beat egg whites until soft peaks form, fold lightly into chocolate mixture. Pour into 2 greased and base-lined round sandwich tins, 20cm in diameter. Bake in moderate oven 20 minutes or until cakes shrink slightly from side of tins. Stand 5 minutes before turning onto wire rack to cool. Join together with whipped cream and strawberries.
■ **TO FREEZE:** Wrap cold, unfilled, cake in freezer wrap to exclude air; freeze for up to 3 months.
Note: This recipe is not suitable to microwave.

Dinner service is Mikasa Dutch Garden.

Make the most of microwaves by cooking a complete dinner party in your microwave oven.

Follow this plan for perfect results.
1. Complete Apricot Swirl Cheese-cake up to a day before party.
2. Complete Parsley Hollandaise Sauce on day of party.
3. Complete Tomato Ginger Coulis on day of party, ready to reheat.
4. Heat Coulis before cooking seafood on skewers;
5. Toast almonds for Brussels Sprouts.
6. Cook Potato and Carrot Pie for required time while guests are eating the first course.
7. Cook chicken for 4 minutes, stand, covered.
8. Cook Brussels Sprouts, stand, covered.
9. Reheat chicken; it will probably take only a minute to cook.
10. Reheat potato pie, if necessary, while placing food on plates.

A MICROWAVE DINNER PARTY FOR SIX

SEAFOOD WITH TOMATO GINGER COULIS
CHICKEN WITH PARSLEY HOLLANDAISE SAUCE
POTATO AND CARROT PIE
BRUSSELS SPROUTS WITH ALMONDS
APRICOT SWIRL CHEESECAKE

SEAFOOD WITH TOMATO GINGER COULIS

Prepare skewers up to 24 hours before serving, brush with butter mixture. The Coulis can be made the day before, store covered in refrigerator, reheat in microwave oven just before serving.

18 green king prawns, shelled
18 scallops
30g butter, melted
2 teaspoons lemon juice
TOMATO GINGER COULIS
3 large (500g) ripe tomatoes, chopped
3 green shallots, chopped
1 small clove garlic, crushed
1 teaspoon grated fresh ginger
1 tablespoon tomato paste
1 teaspoon brown sugar
Cut prawns down back, but not right through, remove vein. Press open gently along cut with side of knife. Cut tough membrane from scallops. Wrap a prawn around each scallop. Skewer 3 prawn-wrapped scallops on each of 6 bamboo skewers. Place skewers in single layer on plate, brush with combined butter and lemon juice, cover, cook on HIGH 1 minute. Turn skewers, brush with remaining butter and lemon juice, cover, cook on HIGH 1 minute. Serve with Tomato Ginger Coulis.
Tomato Ginger Coulis: Combine tomatoes, shallots, garlic and ginger in bowl, cook on HIGH 8 minutes, stirring halfway through cooking time. Push through a sieve, stir in tomato paste and sugar, reheat on HIGH 1 minute.
■ **TO FREEZE:** Seafood on skewers is not suitable to freeze. Coulis can be made, cooled and frozen for 4 weeks.

CHICKEN WITH PARSLEY HOLLANDAISE SAUCE

Make sauce on day of serving, serve at room temperature over hot chicken. Cook chicken as close to serving time as possible; chicken tends to dry out when reheated.

6 chicken breast fillets
1 tablespoon water
PARSLEY HOLLANDAISE SAUCE
1 tablespoon white vinegar
125g butter, chopped
2 teaspoons cornflour
2 teaspoons lemon juice
¼ cup cream
1 egg yolk
1 cup parsley sprigs
Place chicken in single layer in shallow dish, add water, cover, cook on HIGH 6 minutes or until chicken is tender.
Parsley Hollandaise Sauce: Place vinegar in bowl, cook on HIGH 1 minute. Add butter, stir 1 minute, cook on HIGH 30 seconds. Stir in blended cornflour and lemon juice. Cook on HIGH 1 minute, stirring once. Stir in cream, egg yolk and parsley. Puree sauce in blender or processor until smooth.
Note: This recipe is not suitable to freeze.

POTATO AND CARROT PIE
125g lean leg ham
3 large (500g) potatoes, sliced
6 medium (500g) carrots, sliced
6 green shallots, chopped
1 onion, finely sliced
⅓ cup grated parmesan cheese
1 cup milk
1 tablespoon grated orange rind
Cut ham into strips. Arrange layers of potato, carrot, ham, shallots, onion and cheese in alternate layers in a round shallow dish, 20cm in diameter. Pour combined milk and orange rind over vegetables, cover, cook on HIGH 15 minutes or until vegetables are tender.
Note: This recipe is not suitable to freeze.

China is Kayser Rio.

BRUSSELS SPROUTS WITH ALMONDS
500g brussels sprouts
2 tablespoons flaked almonds
30g butter
Place butter and almonds in bowl, cook on HIGH 2 minutes or until almonds are lightly toasted, stirring once during cooking. Place trimmed sprouts in shallow dish, cover, cook on HIGH 5 minutes or until tender, toss with almonds and butter.
Note: This recipe is not suitable to freeze.

APRICOT SWIRL CHEESECAKE

Cheesecake can be made the day before and refrigerated until required.

185g packaged sweet biscuits, crushed
90g butter
FILLING
250g packet cream cheese, softened
⅓ cup sour cream
2 eggs
⅓ cup castor sugar
2 teaspoons grated lemon rind
¼ cup lemon juice
425g can apricot halves, drained
2 passionfruit
300ml carton thickened cream, whipped
Melt butter in dish on HIGH 1 minute; add biscuit crumbs, press over base and side of pie plate (base measures 18cm). Cook on HIGH 1 minute, cool. Pour cream cheese mixture into crumb crust, drizzle with apricot mixture, swirl through gently with knife. Cook on MEDIUM HIGH 5 minutes, stand 3 minutes, cook on MEDIUM HIGH 5 minutes, cool, refrigerate until firm. Decorate with cream and remaining passionfruit.
Filling: Beat cream cheese and sour cream until smooth, add eggs, sugar, lemon rind and juice, beat well. Blend or process apricots until smooth, stir in half the passionfruit.
■ **TO FREEZE:** Prepare, cover, freeze for up to 2 weeks.

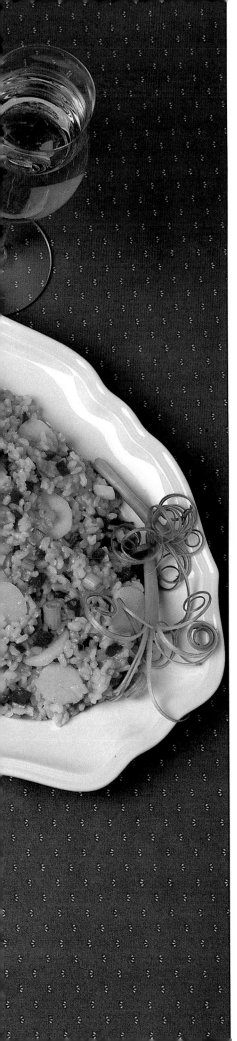

The food we've chosen for this menu takes very little time to prepare; some can be done ahead.

QUICK 'N' EASY DINNER PARTY FOR FOUR

PRAWNS AND CAMEMBERT WITH AVOCADO CREAM

CHICKEN FILLETS WITH APRICOT GINGER SAUCE

CRUNCHY SWEET AND SOUR RICE

SNOW PEAS IN GARLIC MINT BUTTER

SWISS CHOCOLATE MOUSSE

PRAWNS AND CAMEMBERT WITH AVOCADO CREAM

Prepare Avocado Cream as close to serving time as possible.

3 avocados
2 tablespoons lemon juice
1 tablespoon oil
¼ cup cream
2 tablespoons mayonnaise
12 cooked king prawns, shelled
125g packet camembert cheese
1 lettuce

Peel and stone avocados. Puree 2 of the avocados in blender or processor with lemon juice, oil, cream and mayonnaise. Slice remaining avocado, arrange with slices of cheese and prawns on lettuce, serve topped with avocado cream.
Note: This recipe is not suitable to freeze.

SNOW PEAS IN GARLIC MINT BUTTER

Prepare snow peas up to a day in advance; keep refrigerated.

200g snow peas
30g butter
2 cloves garlic, crushed
1 teaspoon chopped mint

Top and tail snow peas. Melt butter in pan, add garlic and mint. Stir in peas, saute until just tender.
■ **TO MICROWAVE:** Combine all ingredients in large shallow dish, cook on HIGH 5 minutes or until peas are just tender.
Note: This recipe is not suitable to freeze.

CHICKEN FILLETS WITH APRICOT GINGER SAUCE

Sauce can be made a day before required. Chicken is best cooked just before serving to prevent drying out.

4 large chicken breast fillets
30g butter
2 tablespoons oil
APRICOT GINGER SAUCE
3cm piece green ginger, peeled
425g can apricot nectar
3 teaspoons soy sauce
2 teaspoons cornflour
1 tablespoon water
1 green shallot, sliced

Heat butter and oil in pan, add chicken, cook about 10 minutes or until golden brown on both sides and tender. Remove from pan, place on serving dish, top with Sauce. Cover, keep warm in oven for up to 10 minutes.
Apricot Ginger Sauce: Make Sauce while chicken is cooking. Cut ginger into wafer-thin slices, then into shreds. Combine apricot nectar, ginger and soy sauce in pan, bring to boil, stir in blended cornflour and water, stir until Sauce boils and thickens, add shallot.
■ **TO MICROWAVE:** Melt butter in shallow dish (omit oil) on HIGH 1 minute, add chicken, coat in butter, cover with plastic food wrap, cook on HIGH 5 minutes or until chicken is tender. Place on serving dish, top with Sauce.
Apricot Ginger Sauce: Cut ginger into wafer-thin slices, then into shreds. Combine apricot nectar, ginger and soy sauce in bowl, cook on HIGH 5 minutes, add blended cornflour and water, cook on HIGH 2 minutes or until sauce boils and thickens, add shallot.

Dinner service is Villeroy and Boch Manoir; glasses are Orrefors Lisa.

CRUNCHY SWEET AND SOUR RICE

Prepare Sauce in the morning, reheat when required. We cooked 2 cups of rice for this recipe; cook it in advance and reheat over simmering water.

4 cups cooked brown rice
1 small red pepper, chopped
2 green shallots, chopped
$\frac{1}{3}$ cup canned water chestnuts, sliced
SWEET AND SOUR SAUCE
1 tablespoon cornflour
$\frac{1}{2}$ cup chicken stock
$\frac{1}{2}$ cup canned pineapple juice
1$\frac{1}{2}$ tablespoons white vinegar
2 teaspoons sugar
1 tablespoon peanut butter

Combine hot rice with pepper, shallots and water chestnuts. Stir in hot Sweet and Sour Sauce, serve immediately.

Sweet and Sour Sauce: Blend cornflour with stock. Add pineapple juice, vinegar, sugar and peanut butter. Stir over heat until mixture boils and thickens; reduce heat, simmer 1 minute.

■ **TO FREEZE:** Cooked rice freezes well for up to 2 months; the rest of the recipe is not suitable to freeze.

■ **TO MICROWAVE:** Combine ingredients for Sauce in bowl, cook on HIGH 3 minutes, or until Sauce boils and thickens.

SWISS CHOCOLATE MOUSSE

Make the Mousse up to 2 days before required, if preferred; store covered in refrigerator.

100g block Toblerone chocolate, chopped
2 eggs, separated
$\frac{1}{2}$ cup thickened cream

Melt chocolate in large bowl over hot water. Use a wooden spoon to mix in egg yolks, one at a time; beat until smooth and thick. Fold in whipped cream, then softly beaten egg whites. Spoon into individual serving dishes ($\frac{1}{2}$-cup capacity) refrigerate several hours or until firm. Decorate with extra whipped cream, strawberries and chocolate curls if desired.

■ **TO MICROWAVE:** Melt chocolate in bowl on HIGH 1 minute. Proceed with recipe as above.

Note: This recipe is not suitable to freeze.

This is a great way to entertain friends, either indoors or out. Open sandwiches are easy to prepare, attractive to look at and good to eat.

A LUNCH OF OPEN SANDWICHES FOR 10

FLAVORED BUTTERS

Here are four suggestions for flavored butters. Be generous when buttering the bread to help keep the bread moist and to hold the toppings in position, and, of course, to add flavor. These butters can be made 2 weeks ahead of time and kept covered and refrigerated.

GARLIC AND PARSLEY
250g unsalted butter
2 cloves garlic, crushed
⅓ cup finely chopped parsley

HORSERADISH AND CHIVE
250g unsalted butter
1 tablespoon horseradish cream
2 tablespoons finely chopped chives

BASIL AND LEMON
250g unsalted butter
1 teaspoon finely grated lemon rind
⅓ cup finely chopped basil (or 1 teaspoon dried basil leaves)

GREEN PEPPERCORN AND MUSTARD
250g unsalted butter
3 teaspoons drained canned green peppercorns
1 teaspoon french mustard

Beat softened butter until light and creamy, stir in herbs and seasonings.
■ **TO FREEZE:** Place flavored butter on a piece of foil. Fold foil over butter, shape into a log with the straight side of a knife, roll up, tuck ends under, freeze for up to 2 months.

Most open sandwiches benefit from the addition of a little mayonnaise or sauce of some kind to help hold the toppings in position and to add to the flavor. Try our Cranberry Port Sauce with cold meat — particularly turkey, chicken and lamb — or our Pimiento Bearnaise Sauce with beef or seafood.

CRANBERRY PORT SAUCE

Cranberry sauce is an imported product available from delicatessens and gourmet sections of supermarkets.

½ cup bottled cranberry sauce
1 tablespoon port
1 teaspoon grated orange rind
½ teaspoon french mustard
Combine all ingredients in pan, stir over heat until well blended. Cool, refrigerate, covered, until ready to use.
Makes about ½ cup.
■ **TO FREEZE:** Freeze for up to 1 month in airtight container.
■ **TO MICROWAVE:** Combine all ingredients in bowl, cook on HIGH 2 minutes, or until heated through.

From left: Basil and Lemon; Horseradish and Chive; Garlic and Parsley; Green Peppercorn and Mustard.

PIMIENTO BEARNAISE SAUCE

Pimientos are canned or bottled sweet red peppers. They are an imported product and available in supermarkets and delicatessens. Remaining pimientos can be stored, covered, in the refrigerator for at least 2 months.

2 tablespoons water
2 tablespoons white vinegar
1 green shallot, chopped
250g butter, chopped
4 egg yolks
1 small whole (60g) canned pimiento, drained
Combine water, vinegar and shallot in pan, bring to boil, boil until reduced by half; strain, discard shallot. Melt butter over low heat, cool. Place egg yolks and vinegar mixture in top of double saucepan, whisk in butter gradually over simmering water until mixture thickens. Puree pimiento in blender or processor, slowly pour in Bearnaise Sauce, process until combined.
Makes about 1 cup.
Note: This recipe is not suitable to freeze or microwave.

Look at the photograph for ideas for what to use for open sandwiches and how to use the ingredients for maximum appeal. Below is a list of topping ideas, but let your imagination loose and create your own. Allow three open sandwiches per person, unless your guests are all men with large appetites. Serve our two suggested desserts to complete the meal.

Open sandwiches should be served with a knife and fork, but this means chairs, so, if there is standing room only, make sure the toppings you choose are portable and cut into manageable sizes. Buy a variety of sliced bread. Choose firm bread, such as rye, pumpernickel, wholemeal, etc. Avoid soft doughy breads; they will not support the weight of the toppings. Assemble the sandwiches as close to serving time as possible, have the bread buttered and covered, the toppings ready and covered and preferably have someone to help you prepare them.

Make use of cress, parsley, basil, caviar, tiny lemon or lime wedges, cherry tomatoes, etc., to garnish sandwiches.

SUGGESTED TOPPINGS
Chicken
Rare roast beef
Roast pork
Cold roast lamb
Salami
Ham
Turkey
Canned salmon, tuna
Oysters, mussels
Prawns
Lobster
Rollmops
Smoked salmon, eel, oysters, etc.
Cheese
Eggs, hard boiled, scrambled
Canned pimientos
Gherkins, capers, olives
Fruit
Avocado
Alfalfa sprouts
Asparagus
Mushrooms
Onion rings
Salad vegetables
Watercress, mustard cress

A super selection of decorative and delicious open sandwiches.

MOCHA MOUSSE ROLL

It is true that this recipe does not contain flour. The "cake" is like a deflated souffle with the texture of a mousse; it's delicious and melts in the mouth. Make cake completely the day before required, if desired.

125g dark chocolate, chopped
1 tablespoon instant coffee powder
2 tablespoons boiling water
4 eggs, separated
¾ cup castor sugar
cocoa
300ml carton thickened cream, whipped
COFFEE CREAM
2 teaspoons instant coffee powder
1 tablespoon boiling water
1 tablespoon Tia Maria of Kahlua
300ml carton thickened cream, whipped

Melt chocolate over hot water, stir in combined coffee and water, cool to room temperature. Beat egg yolks and sugar in small basin with electric mixer for 5 minutes or until thick and lemon colored, beat in chocolate mixture. Transfer mixture to large basin. Beat egg whites until soft peaks form, fold into chocolate mixture. Pour into greased and lined swiss roll tin (base measures 25cm x 30cm), bake in moderate oven 12 minutes. Cover with damp cloth until cool, turn out onto greaseproof paper which has been lightly dusted with sifted cocoa. Spread with Coffee Cream, roll up like a swiss roll from the short side (see photograph below). Place roll seam side down, onto serving dish, refrigerate. Spread with cream, decorate with strawberries and chocolate curls, if desired.

Coffee Cream: Combine coffee and water, add Tia Maria, cool to room temperature. Fold into cream.

Note: This recipe is not suitable to freeze or microwave.

Opposite page: Creamy Berry Flan.
Below: Mocha Mousse Roll.
Glass platter is Archimedes by Riedel.

CREAMY BERRY FLAN

We used a pretty fluted rectangular cake tin with a removable base — these tins are available in specialty cookware shops. A large lamington tin would be a good substitute. We used strawberries on our flan; any berry or combination of berries would be delicious. The pastry case can be made a week in advance and stored in an airtight container. Assemble the flan up to 24 hours before serving.

PASTRY
¾ cup plain flour
½ cup self raising flour
2 tablespoons custard powder
2 tablespoons icing sugar
1 teaspoon finely grated orange rind
125g cold butter, chopped
1 tablespoon iced water, approximately
FILLING
2 x 300ml cartons thickened cream
⅓ cup icing sugar
¼ cup Kirsch
1½ tablespoons apricot jam
2 × 250g punnets strawberries, halved
30g dark chocolate, chopped
STEP 1
Combine sifted dry ingredients with orange rind in bowl; rub in butter. Add enough water to bind together, knead on lightly floured surface until smooth; wrap in plastic food wrap, refrigerate 30 minutes. Roll pastry between 2 sheets of plastic food wrap, large

enough to line a rectangular tin with removable base (base measures 20cm x 28cm). Trim edges, line pastry with greaseproof paper, fill with beans or rice, bake in moderate oven 20 minutes, remove paper and beans, bake further 10 minutes, cool on wire rack 15 minutes, remove from tin, cool.

STEP 2
Brush base of pastry with warmed, sieved apricot jam. Beat cream with sifted icing sugar and Kirsch until soft peaks form. Spread cream evenly into pastry case, arrange halved strawberries on top.

STEP 3
Melt chocolate over hot water, place into piping bag (see pictures on page 11). Pipe chocolate over strawberries, refrigerate 15 minutes or until chocolate is set.

Note: This recipe is not suitable to freeze or microwave.

The low joule dinner party for four dieters is a delight to look at and great to eat. The kilojoule count is low, the total intake is under 3000kJ per person for the three courses.

LOW JOULE DINNER PARTY FOR FOUR

FRESH WATERCRESS SOUP

RACK OF LAMB WITH TASTY VEGETABLE SAUCE

CRUNCHY SALAD WITH CUCUMBER DRESSING

MERINGUE PEARS IN CHOCOLATE SAUCE

FRESH WATERCRESS SOUP

This soup can be made the day before serving, cool, cover, refrigerate overnight. Use water and 2 chicken stock cubes, if desired. You will need 2 bunches watercress for approximately 3 cups coarsely chopped watercress. We used light sour cream and freshly grated nutmeg to top the soup

1 small onion, chopped
4 green shallots, chopped
1 clove garlic, crushed
2 potatoes, peeled, chopped
4 cups chicken stock
3 cups coarsely chopped watercress
1 tablespoon dry powdered potato

Combine onion, shallots, garlic, potatoes and stock in pan, cover, bring to boil, reduce heat, simmer, covered, for 15 minutes, or until potatoes are tender. Add watercress, simmer 5 minutes. Puree soup and powdered potato in batches in blender or processor until soup is smooth. Reheat, serve topped with a little sour cream and nutmeg, if desired.

■ **TO FREEZE:** Cool soup, pour into container, seal, freeze up to 2 months. Reheat gently without boiling.

■ **TO MICROWAVE:** Combine onion, shallots, garlic and potatoes in bowl, cover, cook on HIGH 5 minutes. Add stock and watercress, cover, cook on HIGH 5 minutes. Proceed as above.

About 420kJ per serve.

CRUNCHY SALAD WITH CUCUMBER DRESSING

We used the seedless cucumber for this recipe. It is called the Telegraph or Lebanese cucumber.

2 sticks celery, sliced
1 red apple, sliced
1 small red pepper, chopped
4 green shallots, chopped
2 oranges, segmented
CUCUMBER DRESSING
½ long green seedless cucumber
½ cup low fat yoghurt
1 tablespoon cream

Combine celery, apple, pepper, shallots and orange segments, stir in Dressing just before serving.

Dressing: Blend or process cucumber with yoghurt and cream until smooth.

440 kJ per serve.

RACK OF LAMB WITH TASTY VEGETABLE SAUCE

Be sure to trim all fat from lamb; lamb and vegetables can be prepared a day before serving.

1 rack of lamb (8 chops)
½ x 40g packet French Onion Soup Mix
1½ cups water
1 tablespoon lemon juice
1 medium carrot
2 medium zucchini
1 teaspoon cornflour
2 teaspoons water, extra
2 tablespoons chopped parsley

Cook lamb on rack in baking dish in moderately hot oven for 25 minutes. Combine soup mix, water and lemon juice in pan, bring to boil, reduce heat, simmer uncovered 10 minutes. Cut carrot and zucchini into thin strips about 5cm in length. Bring pan of water to boil, add vegetables, cook 1 minute; drain, add vegetables to sauce. Stir in blended cornflour and extra water, stir over heat until sauce boils and thickens; add parsley, serve over lamb.

■ **TO MICROWAVE:** Place lamb in shallow ovenproof dish, pour combined soup mix, water and lemon juice over lamb; cook on HIGH 12 minutes. Remove lamb, cover with foil to keep warm. Add prepared vegetables and blended cornflour and extra water, cook on HIGH 2 minutes stirring once; add parsley.

Note: This recipe is not suitable to freeze.

About 1470kJ per serve.

MERINGUE PEARS IN CHOCOLATE SAUCE

Prepare pears, almonds and Sauce up to 12 hours before required. Make meringue and bake pears as close to serving time as possible.

2 x 420g cans pears (with no added sugar)
1 tablespoon flaked almonds
2 egg whites
1 tablespoon castor sugar
CHOCOLATE SAUCE
½ teaspoon cocoa
2 tablespoons dry white wine
1 teaspoon arrowroot

Toast almonds on oven tray in moderate oven for about 5 minutes. Drain pears, reserve ¾ cup liquid for Chocolate Sauce. Place pears cut side down in single layer in ovenproof dish. Beat egg whites in small bowl with electric mixer until soft peaks form, add sugar, beat until dissolved. Coat each pear with meringue, bake in moderate oven 10 minutes or until light golden brown. Serve 2 to 3 pears per person, pour Chocolate Sauce around pears, sprinkle with toasted almonds.

Chocolate Sauce: Place cocoa, wine and ½ cup of the reserved liquid in pan, heat until almost boiling. Blend arrowroot with remaining reserved liquid, add to Sauce, stir until Sauce boils and thickens slightly.

About 400kJ per serve.

Note: This recipe is not suitable to freeze or microwave.

Dinner service is Villeroy and Boch Trio; glasses are Orrefors Blanche.

Many people are cutting down on or giving up meat. This dinner party menu is tasty and filling and will satisfy most vegetarians' requirements.

VEGETARIAN DINNER PARTY FOR SIX

CURRIED PEA AND APPLE SOUP

DEEP DISH VEGETARIAN PIZZA

GREEN VEGETABLE SALAD

BAKED CARROT PUDDINGS WITH WHIPPED CITRUS SAUCE

CURRIED PEA AND APPLE SOUP

Prepare soup up to two days in advance, store covered in refrigerator. Use stock reserved from vegetable cooking for tasty results.

30g butter
1 onion, chopped
2 teaspoons curry powder
2 Granny Smith apples, peeled, chopped
2 cups (250g) frozen peas
½ lettuce, shredded
3 cups vegetable stock
½ cup milk

Heat butter in pan, add onion and curry powder. Cook stirring for 2 minutes. Add apples, peas, lettuce and stock, bring to the boil, reduce heat, simmer 10 minutes or until peas are tender. Puree in processor or blender in batches until smooth. Add milk, reheat before serving.
■ **TO FREEZE:** Freeze in sealed container for up to 2 months.
■ **TO MICROWAVE:** Place butter and onion in bowl, cook on HIGH 3 minutes, add curry powder, cook on HIGH 30 seconds. Add apples, peas, lettuce and stock, cook on HIGH 10 minutes, puree in blender or processor, add milk. Reheat before serving.

DEEP DISH VEGETARIAN PIZZA

Pizza dough can be made, placed into tins and frozen for up to a month. Prepare ingredients for filling up to 12 hours before assembling. Pizzas can be assembled and refrigerated up to 30 minutes before baking.

200g mushrooms sliced
3 small zucchini, grated
⅓ cup tomato paste
½ teaspoon dried oregano leaves
1 onion, chopped
400g can artichoke hearts, drained, chopped
2 cups grated tasty cheese
½ cup pinenuts
2 medium tomatoes, sliced
12 black olives, pitted, halved
PIZZA DOUGH
2 cups plain flour
7g sachet dried yeast
1 teaspoon sugar
¾ cup warm water

Combine mushrooms and zucchini in pan, cover, cook over low heat until tender, drain, press out excess liquid. Toast pinenuts on oven tray in moderate oven for 5 minutes. Spread each pizza base with combined tomato paste and oregano. Top each with onion, artichokes, half the cheese, mushroom mixture, pinenuts, tomatoes and olives. Top with remaining cheese, bake in moderate oven 40 minutes or until golden brown.
Pizza Dough: Sift flour into bowl, add combined yeast, sugar and water, mix to a firm dough. Knead on lightly floured surface for 10 minutes or until smooth and elastic. Divide in half, roll out to cover base and sides of 2 x 18cm sandwich tins.
Note: This recipe is not suitable to freeze or microwave.

Dinner service is Royal Doulton Southdown.

GREEN VEGETABLE SALAD

Vegetables and Dressing can be prepared up to 12 hours before serving. We used Paul Newman's Own Classic Salad Dressing as french dressing for this recipe.

250g green beans
250g asparagus
250g broccoli flowerets
DRESSING:
2 tablespoons french dressing
2 tablespoons lemon juice
¼ teaspoon sesame oil
1 teaspoon grated fresh ginger
1 teaspoon soy sauce

Cut beans and asparagus into 3cm pieces; add vegetables to pan of boiling water, boil 3 minutes or until bright green and just tender, drain, rinse under cold water until completely cold. Place into salad bowl, refrigerate until ready to serve. Add Dressing just before serving.

Dressing: Combine all ingredients.

■ **TO MICROWAVE:** Place prepared vegetables in shallow dish, cover with ¼ cup water and plastic food wrap, cook on HIGH 5 minutes or until bright green and just tender, drain, rinse under cold water until completely cold. Continue as above.

Note: This recipe is not suitable to freeze.

BAKED CARROT PUDDINGS WITH WHIPPED CITRUS SAUCE

These puddings can be prepared the day before, up to the step of baking, covered and refrigerated overnight or can be covered and frozen for up to 2 weeks. Thaw and bake as directed below. Sauce can be made a day ahead of serving time. Any leftover Sauce can be frozen and served as a delicious icecream with fresh fruit.

1 cup finely grated carrot
½ cup sultanas
½ cup currants
½ cup chopped dates
1 tablespoon mixed peel
½ cup water
½ cup brown sugar, firmly packed
90g butter
½ teaspoon bicarbonate of soda
1 egg, lightly beaten
½ cup wholemeal plain flour
½ cup white self raising flour
½ teaspoon mixed spice
1 tablespoon lemon juice or rum
WHIPPED CITRUS SAUCE
4 egg yolks
⅓ cup icing sugar
¼ cup orange juice
300ml carton thickened cream, whipped
2 tablespoons lemon juice or rum

Combine carrot, dried fruit, water, sugar and butter in pan. Bring to boil, simmer, covered 5 minutes, remove from heat, stir in soda; cool to room temperature. Stir in egg, sifted flours, spice and lemon juice. Divide mixture between 6 x 1-cup individual dishes. Place on oven tray. Bake in moderate oven for 30 minutes. Serve warm with Whipped Citrus Sauce.

Whipped Citrus Sauce: Beat egg yolks and sifted icing sugar in small bowl with electric mixer for 5 minutes, or until thick and creamy. Gradually beat in orange juice. Fold cream and lemon juice into egg mixture. Refrigerate, covered, until serving time.

■ **TO MICROWAVE:** Combine first 8 ingredients in large bowl, cook on HIGH 8 minutes or until mixture boils. Stir in soda; cool, proceed as above. Fill dishes with mixture, cover loosely with plastic food wrap, microwave on HIGH 2 minutes or until just firm.

Note: This recipe, once baked, is not suitable to freeze.

DELICIOUS DETAILS

CRYSTALLISED VIOLETS

Violets are edible, and look pretty as a decoration. What's more, they will keep for months if made and stored in an airtight container.

Color the sugar mauve for best results. The easiest, neatest way is to put some castor sugar into a plastic bag, add a few drops of purple or violet food coloring and use your hand to work the coloring through the sugar. Any excess sugar can be stored in an airtight jar for months for some future use.

Choose fresh dry violets, use a fine artist's brush to paint petals sparingly but evenly all over both sides with a little egg white. If you are heavy-handed with the egg white or sugar the violets will droop under the weight and not dry out properly. Now sprinkle the violets evenly, but sparingly, on both sides with the colored sugar. Place the violets on a wire rack in a dry place until the flowers look quite dry; time will depend on the weather. If the weather is wet or humid, the violets can be dried in front of an open oven, with the temperature turned to very slow. Once the flowers are dry, layer them between tissue paper in a container, seal until required.

CHOCOLATE IVY LEAVES

If the chocolate leaves have to maintain a shape at room temperature, use a compound cooking chocolate for best results, but if the leaves are to be used on a dessert or cake, which is refrigerated up to about an hour before serving, then the regular dark chocolate will give excellent results.

Melt chocolate over hot water. Be careful not to overheat, and do not allow any water near the chocolate or it will be ruined. Allow chocolate to cool, but not set; time depends on room temperature. Choose well shaped, suitably sized ivy leaves, wash and dry them thoroughly before using. Use a fairly thick artist's brush to brush chocolate evenly over the back of the leaves; refrigerate until set. When chocolate is set, peel leaves away from chocolate, store chocolate leaves covered in the refrigerator until ready to use. Leaves made from compound chocolate can be stored indefinitely at room temperature.

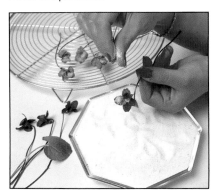

Entertain someone special with this simple, impressive menu.

SPECIAL DINNER PARTY FOR TWO

PARMESAN PRAWNS WITH BASIL DRESSING

BEEF FILLET ON MUSTARD CROUTONS

ASPARAGUS BEAN BUNDLES

HONEY SESAME CARROTS

MINI APPLE PASTRIES

PARMESAN PRAWNS WITH BASIL DRESSING

Prawns can be prepared and refrigerated up to 24 hours before the party. Toss in cheese just before cooking. Prepare Dressing up to a few hours in advance. If possible use freshly grated parmesan cheese. If basil is out of season, substitute parsley. Serve with lettuce (we used the cos variety), cherry tomatoes and lemon wedges.

375g green king prawns
**½ cup (60g) grated parmesan
  cheese**
60g butter
¼ cup oil
BASIL DRESSING
⅓ cup olive oil
1 tablespoon white vinegar
½ teaspoon sugar
¼ cup finely chopped basil
**1 tablespoon grated parmesan
  cheese**

Shell prawns, leaving tails intact, remove back vein, flatten prawns with rolling pin. Toss prawns in parmesan cheese. Heat butter and oil in pan, add prawns, cook quickly on both sides until light golden brown; do not overcook or prawns will toughen. Drain on absorbent paper immediately. Serve with Basil Dressing.
Basil Dressing: Combine all ingredients; mix well.
Note: This recipe is not suitable to freeze or microwave.

BEEF FILLET ON MUSTARD CROUTONS

Prepare Mushroom Filling up to several hours before cooking, if desired. Fill steaks and wrap in bacon ready to cook. Have the bread buttered with the mustard mixture ready to toast in the oven to coincide with the cooking of the steaks.

2 thick eye fillet steaks
2 bacon rashers
2 slices bread, cut 1cm thick
2 teaspoons butter
1 teaspoon grainy mustard
oil for frying
MUSHROOM FILLING
15g butter
4 green shallots, chopped
¾ cup chopped mushrooms
1 clove garlic, crushed
2 tablespoons stale breadcrumbs
1 teaspoon grated lemon rind

Cut a pocket in the side of each steak, fill with Mushroom Filling. Wrap each steak in bacon, secure with toothpick. Spread bread with combined butter and mustard, toast on oven tray in moderate oven about 10 minutes. Fry steaks quickly in a little oil until browned well on both sides, reduce heat slightly, cook until done as desired. Remove toothpick; serve steak on the croutons.
Mushroom Filling: Heat butter in pan, add shallots, mushrooms and garlic, cook 5 minutes, stirring constantly, stir in breadcrumbs and lemon rind.
■ **TO MICROWAVE: Mushroom Filling:** Melt butter in bowl on HIGH 1 minute, stir in shallots, mushrooms and garlic, cook on HIGH 3 minutes, stir in breadcrumbs and lemon rind.
Note: This recipe is not suitable to freeze.

ASPARAGUS BEAN BUNDLES

Beans and asparagus can be cooked in the morning, drained, placed in iced water for a few minutes, then drained again. Tie in bundles and refrigerate.

100g green beans
100g asparagus spears
4 chives
30g butter
2 teaspoons lemon juice

Top, tail and string beans. Trim asparagus to same length as beans. Boil or steam beans and asparagus for about 8 minutes or until just tender, drain, place into iced water. Divide vegetables into 2 bundles, secure each bundle with chives. Melt butter in pan, add lemon juice, add vegetables, cover, cook gently until heated through; serve immediately.
■ **TO MICROWAVE:** Place prepared vegetables in shallow dish, cover, cook on HIGH 5 minutes or until just tender. Proceed as above.
Note: This recipe is not suitable to freeze.

HONEY SESAME CARROTS

Carrots can be cooked in the morning, drained, placed into iced water and drained again.

2 carrots, sliced
1 tablespoon sesame seeds
15g butter
2 teaspoons honey

Boil or steam carrots until just tender; drain. Add sesame seeds to pan, stir over heat until lightly browned. Add butter, honey and carrots, stir until heated through.
Note: This recipe is not suitable to freeze or microwave.

Dinner service is Royal Worcester Contessa; glasses are Orrefors Helena.

MINI APPLE PASTRIES

These pastries can be made and baked the day before and reheated uncovered in a moderate oven for 10 minutes, if desired. However, we like them baked just before serving. Prepare pastries in the morning, cover, refrigerate until ready to cook.

1 Granny Smith apple, peeled, finely chopped
1 teaspoon lemon juice
1 tablespoon apricot jam
2 tablespoons ground almonds
1 tablespoon plain flour
¼ teaspoon cinnamon
2 teaspoons butter
1 sheet ready-rolled puff pastry

Combine apples with lemon juice and jam. Combine almonds, flour and cinnamon in bowl, rub in butter, combine with apple mixture.

STEP 1
Cut pastry into 4 even-sized squares. Place apple mixture along centre of each square. Make 8 cuts in the pastry on either side of the apple mixture.

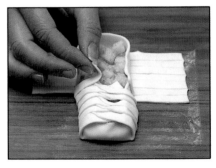

STEP 2
Use top and bottom strips of pastry to enclose filling, divide remaining strips of pastry in half lengthwise.

STEP 3
Place strips of pastry across filling in a criss-cross fashion. Place on lightly greased oven tray, brush with milk, bake in moderately hot oven 10 to 15 minutes or until golden brown. Dust with icing sugar, serve warm with cream.

■ **TO FREEZE:** Prepare pastries as above. Omit brushing with milk. Place uncooked pastries, uncovered, on a tray, freeze several hours, then wrap in freezer wrap or bag. Freeze for up to 2 months. To thaw, place frozen, unwrapped pastries on greased oven tray, brush with milk, bake in moderately hot oven 20 minutes, or until golden brown.
Note: This recipe is not suitable to microwave.

A curry party creates a warm, friendly atmosphere in which to entertain friends and family.

CURRY PARTY FOR 10

MILD PRAWN CURRY

HOT LAMB AND TOMATO CURRY

CURRIED CHICKEN WINGS WITH BANANA
AND COCONUT CREAM

SHREDDED CARROT AND SPROUT SAMBAL

GOLDEN RICE

COCONUT ICECREAM WITH MANGO SYRUP

BUTTERMILK DIAMONDS

When deciding on a curry party, it is important to know the tastes and preferences of family and friends. We have chosen a mild and a hot curry, and one of medium strength. The "heat" of the Hot Lamb and Tomato Curry can be adjusted by increasing, decreasing or even omitting the chilli powder. All the curries tend to be milder rather than hotter. Halve and try the recipes on your family before serving them to guests; this way you can test the "heat" yourself.

Offer a variety of sambals; here are the ones we chose:
Well drained canned corn kernels mixed with chopped red pepper
Sliced red and green apples mixed with raisins
Unpeeled sliced cucumber mixed with plain natural yoghurt and chopped fresh coriander

Mango chutney mixed with fresh mango slices
Sliced bananas with lemon juice and coconut
Roasted salted cashews
Chopped fresh pineapple with finely chopped chilli and mint.
Chopped tomatoes with chopped onion and green shallots
Don't forget pappadams, available from supermarkets. Cook in hot oil for a few seconds.

HOT LAMB AND TOMATO CURRY

Ask butcher to bone out legs of lamb for you or simply cut meat from bone with sharp knife. This recipe can be made up to 2 days ahead; cover, refrigerate. Adjust the amount of chilli powder to suit your taste; the type and age of the chilli powder will affect the heat of the curry. You need 2 tablespoons of the homemade Curry Powder for this recipe; store remaining Curry Powder in airtight container for future use. Keep in cool dark place.

2 × 1½kg legs of lamb, boned
½ cup oil
4 medium onions, chopped
4 cloves garlic, crushed
1 tablespoon grated fresh ginger
2 tablespoons Curry Powder
1 teaspoon chilli powder
4 tomatoes, peeled, chopped
1 cup water.

CURRY POWDER
2 tablespoons blanched almonds
1 teaspoon ground coriander
1 teaspoon dry mustard
1 teaspoon ground cumin
1 teaspoon garam masala
1 teaspoon poppy seeds
½ teaspoon ground fennel
1 teaspoon chilli powder
½ teaspoon ground cardamom
¼ teaspoon ground cloves
¼ teaspoon ground nutmeg
½ teaspoon ground black pepper
½ teaspoon turmeric

Trim fat from lamb, cut lamb into cubes. Heat oil in large pan, add onions, garlic and ginger, cook stirring until lightly browned. Add half the lamb in single layer to pan, cook stirring until well browned, remove from pan. Brown the rest of the lamb in the same way. Return lamb to pan, add 2 tablespoons of the Curry Powder with 1 teaspoon chilli powder, stir over heat 1 minute. Add tomatoes and water to pan, cover, simmer 50 minutes or until lamb is tender.

Curry Powder: Blend all ingredients in blender or processor until fine.

■TO FREEZE: Cool curry to room temperature, place in airtight container, freeze for up to 2 months.
Note: This recipe is not suitable to microwave.

Back row, left to right: Curried Chicken Wings with Banana and Coconut Cream; Golden Rice; Shredded Carrot and Sprout Sambal.
Front Row, left to right: Mild Prawn Curry; Hot Lamb and Tomato Curry.
Handpainted Indian cloths in Curry section are from Robert Morrison Antiques, Woollahra, NSW; china is Apilco from Vasa Agencies; brass bowls are Indian Brass Artwares from Saywell Imports.

SHREDDED CARROT AND SPROUT SAMBAL

Prepare this sambal a day ahead of when required, cover, refrigerate.

4 cups (about 5 medium) grated carrots
2 cups mung bean sprouts
DRESSING
½ cup crunchy peanut butter
½ cup canned coconut milk
¼ cup french dressing
½ teaspoon chilli sauce

Combine carrots and sprouts in large bowl. Add Dressing, toss lightly.
Dressing: Combine all ingredients in screwtop jar; shake well.
Note: This recipe is not suitable to freeze.

MILD PRAWN CURRY

This curry is best made as close to serving time as possible.

STOCK
2kg green king prawns, shelled
**1kg whole white fish (bream or
    schnapper)**
1 onion, chopped
30g butter
1 cup dry white wine
1 litre water
1 bay leaf
1 cup parsley sprigs
CURRY SAUCE
1 onion, chopped
2 sticks celery, chopped
1 clove garlic, crushed
30g butter
¼ cup plain flour
2 teaspoons sugar
1 teaspoon curry powder
½ finely chopped small red chilli
4 tomatoes, peeled, chopped
2 tablespoons tomato paste
1 small red pepper, chopped
1 small green pepper, chopped
250g frozen peas
2 tablespoons chopped coriander
Stock: Devein prawns, reserve half the shells, refrigerate prawns. Fillet fish, reserve head and bones for Stock, remove skin and bones from fillets, cut fish into chunks, refrigerate. Heat butter in pan, add onion, cook stirring few minutes, add reserved prawn shells and fish bones, cook few minutes, add wine, water, bay leaf and parsley. Bring to boil, reduce heat, simmer uncovered 30 minutes; skim often during cooking. Strain Stock, reserve 3 cups for Curry Sauce.

Curry Sauce: Heat butter in pan, add onion, celery and garlic, cook stirring until onion is soft, stir in flour, sugar and curry powder, cook few minutes. Stir in reserved 3 cups Stock and chilli, simmer uncovered 30 minutes. Add tomatoes, tomato paste, peppers, peas, reserved prawns and fish. Simmer few minutes until fish is tender and prawns pink. Sprinkle with coriander just before serving.

Note: This recipe is not suitable to freeze or microwave.

GOLDEN RICE

This rice can be prepared several hours in advance and reheated successfully in the microwave or conventional oven.

1 onion, finely chopped
1 clove garlic, crushed
30g butter
2 cups long grain rice
1 cup dry white wine
3 cups chicken stock
½ teaspoon turmeric
½ cup sultanas
6 green shallots, chopped

Heat butter in large pan, add onion, garlic and rice, cook stirring until rice is coated with butter. Add wine, bring to the boil, add stock and turmeric, cover, cook 20 minutes or until rice is tender. Stir in sultanas and shallots, stand covered 5 minutes before serving

■ **TO FREEZE:** Cook as directed above, omitting sultanas and shallots, cool, freeze in airtight container for 4 weeks. Reheat, stir in sultanas and shallots 5 minutes before serving.

■ **TO MICROWAVE:** Cook onion, garlic and butter in large bowl on HIGH 5 minutes. Add rice, wine, boiling stock and turmeric, cook on HIGH 15 minutes or until rice is tender. Stir in sultanas and shallots, stand covered 5 minutes before serving.

CURRIED CHICKEN WINGS WITH BANANA AND COCONUT CREAM

Chicken wings can be prepared a day ahead; place in the baking dish, cover, refrigerate until cooking time.

2kg chicken wings
1 tablespoon oil
2 large onions, sliced
2 teaspoons curry powder
2 teaspoons ground cumin
½ teaspoon ground fenugreek
½ teaspoon chilli powder
pinch saffron powder
1 clove garlic, crushed
½ × 400ml can coconut cream
1 tablespoon cornflour
1½ cups chicken stock
½ cup thickened cream
4 bananas, sliced
2 tablespoons lemon juice

Fold wing tip under main part of wing. Heat oil in large pan, add onions, cook stirring until golden brown, add curry powder, cumin, fenugreek, chilli and tiny pinch of saffron powder, cook 1 minute stirring. Add garlic and chicken, stir-fry 5 minutes or until chicken is lightly browned. Stir in coconut cream, blended cornflour, stock and cream; stir constantly until mixture boils and thickens. Remove chicken from pan, place into baking dish, pour a little of the sauce over the wings, bake in moderate oven 30 minutes, baste several times during cooking with a little more sauce. Bake further 30 minutes, stir in remaining sauce, bananas and lemon juice, bake further 15 minutes.

■ **TO FREEZE :** This recipe will freeze successfully for up to 2 weeks. Omit banana and lemon juice until reheating. Thaw curry overnight in refrigerator.

Note: This recipe is not suitable to microwave.

COCONUT ICECREAM WITH MANGO SYRUP

2 eggs
2 tablespoons castor sugar
200g white chocolate
400ml can coconut cream
300ml carton thickened cream,
  lightly whipped
MANGO SYRUP
3 mangoes
½ cup sugar
½ cup water
1 tablespoon lemon juice

Whisk eggs and sugar over low heat until frothy. Melt chocolate in bowl over hot water. Whisk chocolate into egg mixture, then whisk in coconut cream. Fold in cream. Pour mixture into loaf tin, cover and freeze. Serve topped with Mango Syrup.

Mango Syrup: Peel mangoes, puree pulp in blender or processor. You will need 2 cups pulp. Dissolve sugar in water over low heat, bring to boil, boil 3 minutes, cool slightly. Add sugar mixture and lemon juice to mangoes, process until combined.

■**TO FREEZE:** Icecream and Mango Syrup can be frozen for up to 2 weeks. Thaw Mango Syrup in refrigerator day before required.

Note: This recipe is not suitable to microwave.

BUTTERMILK DIAMONDS

We used a fluted rectangular cake tin with a removable base — these tins are available in specialty cookware shops. A large lamington tin would be a good substitute. Dessert can be made up to a day before required, if desired; keep covered, refrigerated.

PASTRY
1½ cups plain flour
2 tablespoons icing sugar
125g cold butter, chopped
2 egg yolks
1 tablespoon iced water, approximately
1 egg white
60g blanched almonds
FILLING
125g butter
1½ cups sugar
3 tablespoons plain flour
4 eggs
1 cup buttermilk
2 teaspoons grated lemon rind

Pastry: Combine sifted dry ingredients in bowl, rub in butter. Add egg yolks and enough water to bind together. Knead on lightly floured surface until smooth; wrap in plastic food wrap, refrigerate 30 minutes. Roll Pastry between 2 sheets of plastic food wrap large enough to line a rectangular tin with removable base (base measures 20cm × 28cm). Trim edges, line Pastry with greaseproof paper, fill with beans or rice, bake in moderate oven 15 minutes, remove paper and beans, bake further 10 minutes, cool on wire rack. Brush egg white over base and sides of Pastry, pour in Filling, bake in moderate oven 45 minutes or until just set; cool. Toast almonds on oven tray in moderate oven 5 minutes; cool to room temperature. Cut dessert into diamond shapes, top with toasted almonds.

Filling: Melt butter over low heat. Combine sugar and flour in bowl, stir in butter. Add eggs one at a time, mix well. Stir in buttermilk and lemon rind.

Note: This recipe is not suitable to freeze or microwave.

Opposite page: Coconut Icecream with Mango Syrup.
Below: Buttermilk Diamonds.

Any time is good for a party but if the food can be made well in advance of serving time and served cold, then the hot weather is a good enough excuse to have a celebration at home. The food is special enough to celebrate an engagement, a 21st, an anniversary or just to entertain a group of friends.

SUMMER PARTY FOR 30

SAVORIES

TASTY MINCE PINWHEELS

SMOKED SALMON SLICES

GUACAMOLE WITH PRAWNS

MAIN COURSES

VEAL AND APRICOT TERRINE

CITRUS PORK WITH WILD RICE SEASONING

PEPPERED BEEF WITH TARRAGON BEARNAISE

SALADS

PASTA SALAD WITH SATE DRESSING

MUSHROOM CREAM SALAD

TOMATO BASIL SALAD

DESSERTS

MARZIPAN AND BOYSENBERRY RAINBOW ICECREAM

CREAMY MANGO PAVLOVA

CHOCOLATE CHEESECAKE SLICE

LAYERED MOCHA CAKE

The quantities given all serve 10. If you want to mix and match some hot and cold dishes see our Wedding pages 76 to 80 for some ideas.

The Layered Mocha Cake is a special celebration cake, suitable for any happy occasion.

From back: Tasty Mince Pinwheels; Guacamole with Prawns; Smoked Salmon Slices.
Champagne flutes are Gold Line by Kosta-Boda.

SMOKED SALMON SLICES
2 small bread sticks
250g packet cream cheese
1 tablespoon lemon juice
100g smoked salmon
3 green shallots, finely chopped
Cut ends from bread sticks, remove soft bread from centre without breaking crust. Blend or process cheese and lemon juice until smooth. Add salmon and shallots, blend until smooth. Spoon mixture into bread sticks, wrap in plastic food wrap, refrigerate. Slice when ready to serve.
■ **TO FREEZE:** Wrap bread in freezer wrap, freeze for up to 1 month. Thaw at room temperature for about 6 hours before slicing.

TASTY MINCE PINWHEELS
500g sausage mince
2 teaspoons mango chutney
½ teaspoon curry powder
1 green apple, peeled, grated
1 onion, finely chopped
375g packet frozen puff pastry, thawed
1 egg white
Combine mince, chutney, curry powder, apple and onion in bowl, Roll out half the pastry on lightly floured surface to a 30cm square. Spread half the mince mixture over pastry, leaving a 2.5cm border around edge, roll up like a swiss roll. Brush with egg white. Using a serrated knife, cut roll into 1cm slices. Repeat with remaining pastry and mince mixture. Place slices on oven tray, bake in moderate oven 20 minutes or until golden brown.
Makes 40.
■ **TO FREEZE:** Freeze uncooked in single layer, covered, for up to 4 weeks. Bake while frozen in moderate oven 35 minutes or until golden brown.
Note: This recipe is not suitable to microwave.

GUACAMOLE WITH PRAWNS

Prepare prawns a day before serving, provided they are very fresh. Mix with lemon juice. Keep covered in refrigerator. Make Guacamole on day of serving; keep covered tightly in refrigerator to prevent discoloring.

1kg cooked king prawns
2 tablespoons lemon juice
1 large avocado, chopped
3 green shallots, chopped
2 tablespoons lemon juice, extra
dash tabasco
1 tablespoon sour cream
Shell and devein prawns, combine in bowl with lemon juice. Blend or process avocado and shallots until smooth. Add extra lemon juice, tabasco and sour cream, process until combined, serve with prawns.
Note: This recipe is not suitable to freeze.

CITRUS PORK WITH WILD RICE SEASONING

Pork can be cooked, cooled and refrigerated up to 2 days before serving. Ask butcher to bone out loin of pork for you and to leave a long flap to make it easier to season and roll.

2½kg boned loin of pork
salt
oil
½ cup orange juice
2 tablespoons orange marmalade
1 tablespoon honey
2 teaspoons soy sauce
WILD RICE SEASONING
½ cup wild rice
½ cup brown rice
1 cup (100g) chopped pecan nuts
2 teaspoons butter
1 small onion, finely chopped
1 stick celery, finely chopped
1 clove garlic, crushed
½ cup stale wholemeal breadcrumbs
6 green shallots, chopped
1 teaspoon grated fresh ginger
1 egg, lightly beaten
CITRUS SAUCE
1 orange
1 cup orange juice
¼ cup orange marmalade
2 tablespoons lemon juice
2 teaspoons french mustard
¼ cup water

Remove rind from pork, rub a little salt and oil into rind for crackling. Open loin of pork out flat, place Seasoning along centre of pork. Roll up, secure firmly with string. Place seam side down in baking dish, bake in hot oven 30 minutes or until fat begins to brown. Reduce heat to moderate, bake further 1 hour. Brush with combined orange juice, marmalade, honey and soy sauce, bake further 30 minutes or until pork is tender. Place rind on oven tray, bake on top rack in oven while pork is baking. If crackling has not puffed and browned by the end of the roasting time, place under hot griller for a few minutes. Cool pork to room temperature, wrap in foil, refrigerate overnight. Slice thinly, serve with Citrus Sauce.

Wild Rice Seasoning: Add wild and brown rice to large pan of rapidly boiling water, boil uncovered 30 minutes or until both rices are tender. Toast pecans on oven tray in moderate oven for about 5 minutes. Heat butter in pan, add onion, celery and garlic, saute until onion is soft. Place in large bowl, mix in both rices, breadcrumbs, shallots, ginger, pecans and egg.

Citrus Sauce: Peel orange with vegetable peeler, shred peel finely, drop into pan of boiling water, simmer few minutes, drain. Combine remaining ingredients in pan. Boil uncovered until Sauce reduces by half, strain, add shredded orange.

■**TO FREEZE:** Pork can be seasoned, wrapped and frozen for up to 2 months. Thaw for about 36 hours in refrigerator, cook as above.
Note: This recipe is not suitable to microwave.

PEPPERED BEEF WITH TARRAGON BEARNAISE

Beef can be cooked, covered and refrigerated up to 2 days ahead; slice on the day of serving. Sauce can be cooked in the morning; stand covered at room temperature.

1½ kg piece beef eye fillet
2 tablespoons cracked black peppercorns
1 tablespoon ground cardamom
2 tablespoons oil
TARRAGON BEARNAISE
½ cup tarragon vinegar
10 egg yolks
500g butter

Remove any fat from beef, tie securely with string to hold beef in shape. Roll beef in combined pepper and cardamom. Place oil in baking dish, heat oil and dish well, add beef. Bake in hot oven 20 minutes or until cooked as desired, cool, cover, refrigerate. Slice when cold, serve with Tarragon Bearnaise.

Tarragon Bearnaise: Heat vinegar in pan, simmer until reduced to ⅓ cup, cool. Blend or process egg yolks and vinegar until smooth, gradually pour in hot, bubbly melted butter while blender is operating. Cover, stand at room temperature until required.
Note: This recipe is not suitable to freeze or microwave.

Dinner service: Fitz and Floyd Renaissance design In-Glaze Gray; cutlery, Boda Nova; pork platter, Fitz and Floyd Platine d'Or; terrine platter, Mikasa Scala Gold; tomato salad bowl, Orrefors Eden.

VEAL AND APRICOT TERRINE

Make the terrine at least a day ahead for best results in flavor and cutting. However, terrine can be made a week ahead of the party, cover, refrigerate.

500g veal steak, minced
3 bacon rashers
2 chicken breast fillets
⅓ cup chopped dry apricots
¼ cup dry white wine
30g butter
1 medium onion, chopped
1 clove garlic, crushed
½ cup chopped parsley
2 eggs, lightly beaten
1 cup stale breadcrumbs
1 tablespoon drained canned green
   peppercorns
6 large bacon rashers, extra

Mince or process veal, bacon and chicken finely. Soak apricots in wine for 1 hour; drain, reserve wine. Melt butter in pan, add apricots, onion and garlic, saute few minutes or until onion is soft. Stir in veal, bacon and chicken, then add parsley, eggs, wine, breadcrumbs and peppercorns.

Line base and sides of ovenproof dish or loaf tin (base measures 9cm × 22cm) with extra bacon. Spoon meat mixture into dish, cover top with bacon, then with foil. Place in baking dish with enough hot water to come halfway up sides of dish. Bake in moderate oven 1 hour. Remove dish from water, place a weight on top, cool, refrigerate overnight before serving.
Note: This recipe is not suitable to freeze or microwave.

TOMATO BASIL SALAD

Prepare up to 12 hours before required, keep covered in refrigerator.

6 medium tomatoes, peeled, sliced
2 cucumbers, peeled, sliced
2 medium onions, sliced
¾ cup white vinegar
black pepper
2 tablespoons chopped basil (or 2
   teaspoons dried basil leaves)
Layer tomatoes, cucumbers and onions in shallow dish with vinegar, pepper and basil.
Note: This recipe is not suitable to freeze.

Front, from left: Tomato Basil Salad; Veal and Apricot Terrine; Peppered Beef with Tarragon Bearnaise.
Back, from left: Mushroom Cream Salad; Pasta Salad with Sate Dressing; Citrus Pork with Wild Rice Seasoning.

PASTA SALAD WITH SATE DRESSING

Prepare pasta (including adding oil), vegetables and Dressing up to a day before required. Keep covered in refrigerator. Combine pasta and vegetables up to several hours before serving. Add Dressing just before serving.

500g packet pasta
2 teaspoons oil
250g green beans
1 carrot, sliced
3 green shallots, sliced
1 stick celery, sliced
190g can champignons, drained
1 red pepper, finely chopped
½ cup roasted unsalted peanuts
SATE DRESSING
3 tablespoons smooth peanut butter
1 teaspoon curry powder
½ cup oil
2 tablespoons lemon juice

Add pasta gradually to large pan of boiling water, boil rapidly uncovered 10 minutes or until just tender. Drain pasta, rinse under cold water. Mix oil through pasta with hands. Cut beans in half lengthwise, then into 5cm lengths. Bring pan of water to boil, add beans, cook 2 minutes, add carrot, cook further 1 minute. Drain vegetables, rinse under cold water; drain. Combine pasta and all vegetables, add Dressing and peanuts, toss until combined.
Sate Dressing: Blend peanut butter and curry powder gradually with oil and lemon juice.
Note: This recipe is not suitable to freeze or microwave.

MUSHROOM CREAM SALAD

Make salad 24 hours before serving for best flavor.

1kg baby mushrooms, sliced
3 red peppers, chopped
8 green shallots, chopped
¼ cup lemon juice
300ml carton thickened cream
⅓ cup Paul Newman's Own Dressing
1 clove garlic, crushed

Combine mushrooms, peppers and shallots in large salad bowl. Place lemon juice in bowl of processor. While motor is running add cream gradually, then add dressing and garlic. Process until just combined, pour over mushrooms, mix well, cover, refrigerate until ready to serve.
Note: This recipe is not suitable to freeze.

MARZIPAN AND BOYSENBERRY RAINBOW ICECREAM

Pecan Praline can be made and stored in an airtight container for up to 2 weeks. Any berry of your choice can be used in the icecream.

8 egg yolks
⅔ cup castor sugar
3 × 300ml cartons thickened cream
2 teaspoons vanilla
200g roll marzipan or almond paste
PECAN PRALINE
1 cup castor sugar
1 cup (100g) pecan nuts
BOYSENBERRY FILLING
250g frozen boysenberries, thawed
2 tablespoons icing sugar
1 tablespoon cointreau

Beat egg yolks and sugar in medium bowl with electric mixer until mixture is light and fluffy. Heat 3½ cups of the cream in pan until small bubbles appear around the edges of pan; add vanilla. Gradually stir hot vanilla cream into egg yolks. Place 1½ cups of the cream mixture into a separate bowl. Reserve 1 tablespoon Pecan Praline for decorating. Add remaining coarsely chopped Pecan Praline to remaining cream mixture. Pour half of pecan mixture into a loaf tin (base measures 11cm × 18cm) lined with double thickness of foil over base and extending 5 cm up sides of tin. Freeze until firm. Add Boysenberry Filling to reserved one third of vanilla cream mixture; freeze until required. Roll out half the marzipan large enough to cover frozen pecan layer in loaf tin. Top with boysenberry mixture; freeze until firm. Roll out remaining marzipan, place over frozen boysenberry layer. Top with remaining pecan icecream, freeze overnight. Use foil to help unmould icecream onto serving plate. Decorate with remaining whipped cream and reserved Praline.
Pecan Praline: Place sugar in heavy based pan. Place pan over heat, cook without stirring until sugar is melted and golden brown. Tilt pan occasionally during cooking to dissolve all sugar. Place pecans onto greased tray, pour toffee over nuts; when set, break Praline into pieces, store in airtight container until ready to use.
Boysenberry Filling: Puree berries (and juice), icing sugar and cointreau in blender or processor; strain.
■ **TO FREEZE:** Cover unmoulded icecream with plastic food wrap then with foil, freeze for up to 1 month.

CHOCOLATE CHEESECAKE SLICE

Slice can be cooked up to a day before required, if desired. The amount of butter required for the Biscuit Base could vary a little depending on type of biscuit used. If necessary, add a little more melted butter to bind crumbs.

BISCUIT BASE
250g packet shortbread biscuits, crushed
60g butter, melted
FILLING
100g dark chocolate, chopped
250g packet cream cheese
½ cup castor sugar
3 eggs
¾ cup thickened cream
2 tablespoons Tia Maria or Kahlua
½ cup plain flour, sifted
½ cup chopped pecan nuts

From left: Chocolate Cheesecake Slice; Marzipan and Boysenberry Rainbow Icecream; Creamy Mango Pavlova. Glass plates are Mikasa Scala Gold and Spoons are Kosta-Boda.

Biscuit Base: Combine biscuits and butter, press over base of lamington tin (base measures 16cm × 26cm); refrigerate while preparing Filling.

Filling: Melt chocolate over hot water; cool, do not allow to set. Beat cream cheese and sugar in small bowl with electric mixer, beat until smooth, beat in eggs and cream. Add chocolate, liqueur and flour, beat until smooth. Pour over Biscuit Base, sprinkle with pecan nuts. Bake in slow oven 1 hour; cool to room temperature. Serve topped with whipped cream, sliced strawberries and grated chocolate, if desired.

■ **TO FREEZE:** Wrap Slice securely, freeze for up to 1 month. Thaw at room temperature for about 2 hours.

CREAMY MANGO PAVLOVA

Pavlova can be made and stored in airtight container the day before the party. Mango can be pureed the day before and refrigerated. If fresh mangoes are not available, three cans sliced mangoes, drained, can be used instead. Assemble up to 2 hours before serving, refrigerate.

6 egg whites
1¼ cups castor sugar
3 large ripe mangoes
2 tablespoons Grand Marnier
300ml carton thickened cream

Beat egg whites in medium bowl with electric mixer until soft peaks form. Gradually add sugar, 2 tablespoons at a time, beating well after each addition; beat until sugar is dissolved. Beating should take about 10 minutes. Cut a 25cm circle of foil or parchment paper, place onto greased baking tray. Spread meringue evenly over foil. Bake in very slow oven 1½ hours or until meringue feels firm to touch. Turn oven off, leave door closed, allow pavlova to cool in oven.

Carefully peel away foil, place pavlova onto serving dish. Puree 1 mango (or use 1 drained 425g can mangoes), add Grand Marnier. Whip cream until firm peaks form, fold in mango. Spread over pavlova, decorate with remaining sliced mangoes, kiwi fruit and strawberries, if desired.

LAYERED MOCHA CAKE

Cake layers can be cooked and stored in airtight container up to a day ahead of assembling or wrapped securely and frozen for up to 2 months. Cake can be assembled up to 2 days ahead and refrigerated; this will improve flavor and allow easier cutting. Two swiss roll tins will mean you can bake 2 cake layers at a time so buy or borrow 2 tins. Cake boards are available from cake decorating outlets or make your own by covering a piece of pressed hardboard or similar material measuring about 30cm × 35cm with silver or gold paper, secure with sticky tape.

375g butter, softened
1 teaspoon vanilla
1½ cups castor sugar
6 eggs
2¼ cups self-raising flour
⅓ cup cornflour
⅓ cup cocoa
½ cup milk
1 cup flaked almonds
½ cup rum
COFFEE CREAM
½ cup custard powder
½ cup castor sugar
2 cups milk
2 tablespoons instant coffee powder
¼ cup hot water
500g unsalted butter
½ cup castor sugar, extra
CHOCOLATE ICING
180g dark chocolate, chopped
180g unsalted butter

STEP 1
Cream butter, vanilla and sugar until light and fluffy, add eggs one at a time, beating well after each addition. Fold in combined sifted flour, cornflour and cocoa with milk, in 2 batches. Divide cake mixture into 6 equal portions, spread 1 portion into greased and lined swiss roll tin (base measures 25cm × 30cm). Bake in moderate oven 10 minutes or until lightly browned; if cakes are cooking unevenly, alternate their positions after 5 minutes. Turn onto wire rack to cool. Repeat until you have 6 layers of cooked cake. Spread almonds evenly onto flat oven tray, bake in moderate oven about 5 minutes or until golden brown. Brush layers of cake with rum.

STEP 2

Place 1 layer of cake onto cake board or serving plate, spread with ½ cup of Coffee Cream. Continue layering with Coffee Cream until all cakes are used; do not spread Coffee Cream on top of cake.

STEP 3

Spread top of cake evenly with Chocolate Icing. Reserve about 1½ cups Coffee Cream for piping and writing. Spread remaining Coffee Cream around sides of cake. Press toasted almonds evenly over sides of cake.

STEP 4

Pipe Coffee Cream around base and top of cake with small fluted tube; refrigerate. Decorate with crystallised violets and chocolate ivy leaves (see page 35), use Coffee Cream to pipe a message on top, if desired.

Coffee Cream: Combine custard powder and sugar in pan, blend in milk, stir constantly over heat until mixture boils and thickens, cover surface of mixture with plastic wrap to prevent skin forming, cool, refrigerate. Combine coffee and water, cool. Beat butter and extra sugar in large bowl with electric mixer until light and fluffy, gradually beat in the cold custard and coffee mixture.

Chocolate Icing: Melt chocolate and butter over hot water, cool to room temperature, beat with wooden spoon until thick and spreadable.

The Australian baked dinner is a tradition but we have given it a new twist.

AUSTRALIAN DINNER PARTY FOR 10

PRAWN AND OYSTER PLATTER

CHIVE MAYONNAISE, COCKTAIL SAUCE

ROAST BEEF WITH RED WINE SAUCE

HORSERADISH AND MUSTARD CREAMS

CAULIFLOWER WITH BACON SAUCE

GLAZED PARSNIPS AND CARROTS

GREEN BEANS WITH LEMON

BUTTERED NEW POTATOES

BABY BLUE PUMPKINS WITH RICE

CRUSTY CHEESE DAMPER

TROPICAL TRIFLE

LAMINGTON BAR CAKES

We suggest you serve about 2kg king prawns and 20 to 30 oysters with the Sauce and Mayonnaise for the entree. The beef has two accompaniments; serve one or both. The damper is an optional extra for still-hungry guests. Serve the trifle and cake for dessert, or make two trifles for dessert, and serve the cake with coffee or tea.

CHIVE MAYONNAISE

Mayonnaise can be made up to 2 weeks in advance, store covered in refrigerator. Have eggs and oil at room temperature to prevent curdling. If oil is added too quickly, mayonnaise will curdle. If this should happen, place an extra egg yolk into another bowl, gradually whisk in curdled mixture a little at a time. The extra egg yolk will re-emulsify the mayonnaise.

2 egg yolks
½ teaspoon french mustard
1 tablespoon lemon juice
1 cup oil
2 teaspoons chopped chives
2 teaspoons chopped parsley
2 tablespoons cream, approximately

Clockwise from bottom: Cauliflower with Bacon Sauce; Baby Blue Pumpkins with Rice; Prawn and Oyster Platter with Chive Mayonnaise and Cocktail Sauce; Mustard Cream; Horseradish Cream; Buttered New Potatoes; Glazed Parsnips and Carrots; Crusty Cheese Damper.
In centre: Roast Beef with Red Wine Sauce; Green Beans with Lemon.

STEP 1
Combine egg yolks, mustard and half the lemon juice in small bowl of electric mixer, beat until pale and thick. Gradually add oil in a very thin stream, while mixer is operating on medium speed. Beat until oil is completely absorbed.

STEP 2
When all oil has been added, beat in remaining lemon juice, chives, parsley and enough cream to give smooth consistency.
Note: This recipe is not suitable to freeze.
Makes about 1½ cups.

COCKTAIL SAUCE

This sauce can be made a day before required, if desired. Keep covered in refrigerator.

¼ **cup mayonnaise**
¼ **cup tomato sauce**
1 **tablespoon brandy**
2 **teaspoons worcestershire sauce**
⅓ **cup sour cream**
few drops tabasco sauce
Combine all ingredients in bowl, beat until smooth.
Note: This recipe is not suitable to freeze.

Makes about 1 cup.

Back, left to right: Buttered New Potatoes; Glazed Parsnips and Carrots; Mustard Cream; Horseradish Cream.
Front: Green Beans with Lemon; Roast Beef with Red Wine Sauce.

ROAST BEEF WITH RED WINE SAUCE

Ask butcher for a whole piece of sirloin, boned out; it's a deliciously tender cut. We used the tiny pickling onions for this recipe; if unavailable, peel and coarsely chop 3 large onions instead. Make your own beef stock, or use water and 1 crumbled beef stock cube in this recipe. Cook beef as close to serving time as possible.

2½**kg sirloin beef, boned out**
2 **tablespoons oil**
20 **baby onions, peeled**
2 **tablespoons plain flour**
2 **cups beef stock**
½ **cup red wine**
2 **tablespoons mint jelly**

Heat oil in baking dish, add beef to dish, surround with onions. Bake in moderate oven 1½ hours. Remove meat and onions, keep warm. Drain fat from dish, except for about 2 tablespoons. Sprinkle flour over fat, stir constantly over heat until lightly browned. Gradually stir in stock and wine, stir until sauce boils and thickens. Add mint jelly, stir until melted; strain. Serve hot over sliced beef with Mustard or Horseradish Cream.
Note: This recipe is not suitable to freeze or microwave.

HORSERADISH CREAM

Store Horseradish Cream, covered, in refrigerator for up to 1 week.

150g jar horseradish cream
½ cup sour cream
1 tablespoon lemon juice
Combine all ingredients, mix well.
Note: This recipe is not suitable to freeze.

MUSTARD CREAM

Store Mustard Cream, covered, in refrigerator for up to 5 days.

½ cup french mustard
1 tablespoon grainy mustard
½ cup cream, lightly whipped
1 clove garlic, crushed
1 tablespoon honey
Combine all ingredients, mix well.
Note: This recipe is not suitable to freeze.

VEGETABLE ACCOMPANIMENTS

Prepare vegetables up to a day before cooking. Store covered in refrigerator. Cook as close to serving time as possible.

CAULIFLOWER WITH BACON SAUCE

We used baby cauliflower in this recipe; if unavailable, use 1 large cauliflower cut into large pieces.

1kg cauliflower
4 bacon rashers, chopped
60g butter
¼ cup plain flour
3 cups milk
4 green shallots, chopped
Boil or steam cauliflower until just tender. Melt butter in pan, add bacon, cook stirring until bacon is crisp. Add flour, stir over heat 2 minutes. Add milk gradually, stir constantly over heat until sauce boils and thickens. Serve over cauliflower, sprinkle with shallots.
■ **TO MICROWAVE:** Place cauliflower in single layer in dish, add about ¼ cup water, cover, cook on HIGH for 10 minutes or until cauliflower is tender, drain. Melt butter in bowl, add bacon, cook on HIGH 3 minutes or until crisp. Stir in flour, then milk gradually. Cook on HIGH 4 minutes or until sauce boils and thickens, stir twice during cooking. Pour sauce over cauliflower, reheat on HIGH if necessary. Sprinkle with shallots.
■ **TO FREEZE:** Prepare completely (except for shallots) in ovenproof dish, cool, freeze for up to 4 weeks. When ready to serve, cover with foil, bake in moderate oven about 30 minutes or until heated through. Serve sprinkled with shallots.

GLAZED PARSNIPS AND CARROTS
500g parsnips
500g carrots
30g butter
2 tablespoons honey
Cut parsnips and carrots into finger lengths. Boil or steam until just tender. Drain, return to pan, add butter and honey, cook stirring until well mixed.
■ **TO MICROWAVE:** Place parsnips and carrots in shallow dish, add 1 tablespoon water, cover, cook on HIGH 8 minutes or until just tender. Drain, add butter and honey, cook on HIGH 2 minutes, stir gently.
Note: This recipe is not suitable to freeze.

GREEN BEANS WITH LEMON
1kg green beans
1 tablespoon lemon juice
Top and tail beans. Steam or boil until just tender. Drain, sprinkle with lemon juice just before serving.
■ **TO MICROWAVE:** Top and tail beans, place in shallow dish, sprinkle with 2 tablespoons water, cover, cook on HIGH 8 minutes or until tender. Sprinkle drained beans with lemon juice just before serving.
Note: This recipe is not suitable to freeze.

Back: Baby Blue Pumpkins with Rice.
Front: Cauliflower with Bacon Sauce.

BUTTERED NEW POTATOES

1kg baby new potatoes
30g butter
2 tablespoons chopped parsley

Boil or steam potatoes until tender. Drain, stir in butter and parsley.

■ **TO MICROWAVE:** Place potatoes in shallow dish, add 1 cup water, cover, cook on HIGH 10 minutes or until tender, drain, add butter and parsley.

Note: This recipe is not suitable to freeze.

BABY BLUE PUMPKINS WITH RICE

We used small blue pumpkins. Golden Nuggets or halved Butternut pumpkins can also be used. Pumpkins can be filled a day before required and refrigerated until cooking time.

4 small pumpkins (about 1kg each)
1½ cups brown rice
4 cups chicken stock
30g butter
1 clove garlic, crushed
1 onion, chopped
1 stick celery, chopped
300g can red kidney beans, drained
1 teaspoon dried mixed herbs
1 red pepper, chopped
2 eggs, lightly beaten

Cut small slice from base of each pumpkin so they will sit flat. Cut top from pumpkins, scoop out seeds. Add rice to pan of boiling stock, cover, reduce heat, simmer for 30 minutes or until all stock has been absorbed.

Melt butter in large pan, add garlic, onion and celery, cook stirring until onion is soft. Add rice to pan, stir in well rinsed beans, herbs, pepper and eggs. Spoon mixture into pumpkin shells, replace tops, place in lightly greased baking dish, brush outside of pumpkins lightly with oil, bake uncovered in moderate oven 35 minutes or until pumpkins are just tender.

■ **TO MICROWAVE:** Prepare pumpkins as above. Place stock in large bowl, cover, bring to boil, add rice, cover, cook on HIGH 35 minutes, stir twice during cooking. Cook butter, garlic, onion and celery in shallow dish on HIGH 5 minutes. Stir in well rinsed beans, herbs, pepper, rice and eggs. Spoon into pumpkin shells, replace tops, brush outside of pumpkins lightly with oil, cook on HIGH 15 minutes or until pumpkins are just soft.

Note: This recipe is not suitable to freeze.

CRUSTY CHEESE DAMPER

Damper is best served hot, straight from the oven but can be made in the morning before required and reheated in moderate oven for about 15 minutes.

4 cups self-raising flour
2½ cups milk, approximately
1 cup grated tasty cheese
1 teaspoon dry mustard
1 tablespoon sesame seeds

STEP 1

Sift flour into bowl, stir in enough milk to give a sticky dough. Knead on lightly floured surface until smooth, shape into a round. Place dough onto lightly greased oven tray, press out with fingers to about 3cm thick. Using a sharp knife, mark into 10 wedges, cut wedges into dough about 1cm deep.

STEP 2

Sprinkle dough with combined cheese and mustard, top with sesame seeds. Bake in hot oven 15 minutes, reduce heat to moderately hot, bake further 20 minutes or until golden brown and damper sounds hollow when tapped with fingers.

■ **TO FREEZE:** Cool damper, wrap tightly, freeze for up to 4 weeks. Wrap in foil, bake while frozen, wrapped in foil, in moderate oven for about 30 minutes or until hot.

Note: This recipe is not suitable to microwave.

TROPICAL TRIFLE

Use the fruit — fresh or canned — of your choice to decorate the trifle. The cake, jelly and custard layers of the trifle can be completed, covered and refrigerated up to 2 days ahead of serving time, if desired. Decorate with fruit and whipped cream up to several hours before serving time.

SWISS ROLL
3 eggs, separated
½ cup castor sugar
¾ cup self-raising flour
2 tablespoons hot milk
¾ cup lemon butter
½ cup sweet sherry
2 x 100g packets lemon jelly crystals
CUSTARD
1¼ cups custard powder
1 cup sugar
3 cups milk
300ml carton thickened cream
2 teaspoons vanilla
4 egg yolks

Swiss Roll: Beat egg whites in small bowl with electric mixer until soft peaks form; gradually beat in sugar, beat until dissolved. Beat in egg yolks, transfer mixture to large bowl. Fold in sifted flour and hot milk lightly. Pour mixture into greased and lined swiss roll tin (base measures 25cm x 30cm). Bake in hot oven 8 minutes or until sponge is elastic to touch and lightly browned. While sponge is cooking, place a sheet of greaseproof paper on table; spinkle lightly with extra castor sugar. When sponge is cooked, turn quickly onto paper, peel off lining paper. Cut off crisp edges from long sides. Spread sponge evenly with lemon butter, roll up loosely with the help of the greaseproof paper. Lift roll onto wire rack to cool.

Cut swiss roll into slices, place over base of serving dish. Sprinkle with sherry. Add 1½ cups boiling water to jelly crystals, stir until dissolved, stir in 1½ cups cold water, refrigerate until almost set. Pour jelly over cake, refrigerate until jelly is set. Pour custard over jelly, refrigerate. Decorate with fruit and whipped cream.

Custard: Combine custard powder and sugar in pan, gradually stir in milk and cream. Stir constantly over heat until mixture boils and thickens. Remove from heat, stir in vanilla and egg yolks, cover, cool to room temperature.

Note: This recipe is not suitable to freeze or microwave.

LAMINGTON BAR CAKES

Uniced cakes can be made, cooled and iced up to a day before serving; store in airtight container. Fill up to 12 hours before serving, store covered in refrigerator.

BUTTER CAKE
¾ cup sugar
⅓ cup water
125g butter, softened
1 teaspoon vanilla
3 eggs, separated
1½ cups self-raising flour, sifted

CHOCOLATE GLACE ICING
3 cups icing sugar
⅓ cup cocoa
⅓ cup milk, approximately
1 cup coconut, approximately

MOCK CREAM FILLING
⅔ cup jam
⅓ cup water
½ cup sugar
125g butter, softened
1 teaspoon vanilla

Butter Cake: Combine sugar and water in pan, stir over heat until sugar is dissolved, bring to boil without stirring, remove from heat, cool to room temperature.

Beat butter, vanilla and egg yolks in small bowl with electric mixer until light and creamy, gradually add sugar syrup in a thin stream while mixer is operating. Transfer mixture to a larger basin, stir in flour all at once. Beat egg whites in small bowl with electric mixer until soft peaks form, fold lightly into cake mixture in 2 batches. Divide mixture between 2 well greased bar tins, (base measures 7cm x 25cm). Bake in moderate oven 30 minutes; turn onto wire rack to cool. When cold, spread Chocolate Glace Icing over top and sides of cakes; quickly sprinkle coconut over cakes before Icing is set. Cut piece from top of each cake, spread cavity with jam, fill with Mock Cream, replace top which has been cut in half lengthwise. Decorate with strawberries, if desired.

Chocolate Glace Icing: Sift icing sugar and cocoa into heatproof bowl, stir in enough milk to give thick paste. Stir Icing over hot water until spreadable, spread over one cake at a time. Sprinkle with coconut before icing the next cake; this Icing will set quickly.

Mock Cream Filling: Combine sugar and water in pan, stir over heat until sugar is dissolved, bring to boil without stirring, remove from heat, cool to room temperature. Beat butter and vanilla in small bowl with electric mixer until light and creamy, gradually add sugar syrup in a thin stream while mixer is operating; beat until fluffy.

■ **TO FREEZE:** Cold uniced cakes can be frozen for up to 2 months. Icing and Cream are not suitable to freeze.

Note: This recipe is not suitable to microwave.

Lamington Bar Cakes.
Small plate is Wedgwood Midwinter Sun.

Here's a selection of our favorite goodies to serve with coffee; some are ideal as a dessert, too.

THINGS TO HAVE WITH COFFEE

HAZELNUT ROLL WITH CHESTNUT CREAM

Roll can be completed and refrigerated a day before serving, if desired. Sweetened chestnut spread is available from supermarkets and gourmet delicatessens. Do not confuse with the unsweetened chestnut puree.

1 cup (125g) roasted hazelnuts
5 eggs, separated
¾ cup castor sugar
CHESTNUT CREAM
125g packet cream cheese, softened
½ cup canned sweetened chestnut spread
½ cup thickened cream, whipped
2 teaspoons brandy

Blend or process hazelnuts until finely ground. Beat egg yolks and sugar in small bowl with electric mixer until thick and creamy; stir in hazelnuts. Beat egg whites until firm peaks form, stir ⅓ of egg whites into hazelnut mixture, then fold hazelnut mixture into remaining egg whites. Pour mixture into greased and lined swiss roll tin (base measures 25cm x 30cm). Bake in moderate oven 20 minutes or until just firm to touch. Cool a few minutes in tin before turning onto wire rack covered with greaseproof paper; remove lining paper, roll up cake loosely. Stand few minutes, unroll, cool to room temperature. Spread Chestnut Cream over cake, roll up. Place on plate, decorate with whipped cream and chocolate curls (see page 7), if desired.

Chestnut Cream: Beat cream cheese and chestnut spread in small bowl with electric mixer until smooth. Fold in cream and brandy.

Note: This recipe is not suitable to freeze or microwave.

WALNUT AND ORANGE GATEAU

Assemble cake (except for Grand Marnier Cream) up to a day before required, if desired. Decorate with Grand Marnier Cream, etc., up to 6 hours before serving.

ORANGE CAKE
1 packet sponge cake mix
2 teaspoons grated orange rind
½ cup fresh orange juice
WALNUT MERINGUE CAKES
1¼ cups (125g) walnuts
2 egg whites
½ cup castor sugar
2 tablespoons plain flour, sifted
ORANGE CUSTARD CREAM
4 egg yolks
⅔ cup castor sugar
½ cup cornflour
2 teaspoons grated orange rind
2 cups milk
300ml carton thickened cream, whipped
1 tablespoon Grand Marnier
2 tablespoons icing sugar, sifted
GRAND MARNIER CREAM
300ml carton thickened cream
1 tablespoon Grand Marnier
2 tablespoons icing sugar, sifted

Orange Cake: Make sponge cake according to instructions on packet but replace ½ cup water with the ½ cup of orange juice and add orange rind. Pour into 2 greased 20cm sandwich tins, bake in moderate oven 20 minutes. Turn onto wire rack to cool. When cold, split one cake in half horizontally, freeze other cake for another use. Cover base of a 20cm springform pan with large piece of plastic food wrap. Place half of cake over plastic on base, crust side down. Pull plastic over cake, assemble side of springform pan around edge, clip into place, spread plastic out to line side of pan. Spread ⅓ (about 1 cup) of the Orange Custard Cream over cake, top with 1 Walnut Meringue layer, crusty side up. Spread with another ⅓ of the Orange Custard Cream; top with second layer of cake, crusty side down. Spread with remaining Orange Custard Cream, top with remaining Walnut Meringue layer. Cover with edges of plastic food wrap, refrigerate overnight. Release sides of pan, remove cake, pull plastic food wrap away from sides; invert cake onto serving plate. Remove base of pan and plastic. Spread top and side of cake with Grand Marnier Cream; decorate with orange segments (see page 117) and walnuts, if desired.

Walnut Meringue Cakes: Grind walnuts finely in blender or processor. Beat egg whites until soft peaks form, add sugar gradually, beat until dissolved, fold in combined walnuts and flour. Spread meringue mixture over 2 greased and floured bases of 20cm springform pans. If only one base is available, bake one first, then the other. Bake meringues in moderately slow oven 20 minutes, cool on base 5 minutes, loosen with spatula, turn onto foil-covered wire rack; cool.

Orange Custard Cream: Beat egg yolks and sugar in small bowl with electric mixer until pale and thick, beat in cornflour and orange rind, then gradually add milk, beat until smooth. Pour mixture into pan, stir constantly over heat until mixture boils and thickens. Cool to lukewarm, fold in cream, Grand Marnier and icing sugar.

Grand Marnier Cream: Whip combined cream, Grand Marnier and icing sugar until soft peaks form.

Note: This recipe is not suitable to freeze or microwave.

ALMOND CHOCOLATE WEDGES

Make cake up to a day before required, if desired; coat with Chocolate Glaze on day of serving.

½ cup ground almonds
⅓ cup blanched almond kernels, toasted
125g unsalted butter
60g dark chocolate, chopped
¾ cup castor sugar
½ cup water
1 egg
¼ cup sour cream
½ cup self-raising flour
½ cup plain flour
MOCHA BUTTERCREAM
60g dark chocolate
3 egg yolks
¼ cup sugar
¼ cup water
125g unsalted butter
½ teaspoon instant coffee powder
2 teaspoons hot water
CHOCOLATE GLAZE
125g dark chocolate, chopped
60g butter
2 cups icing sugar, sifted
⅓ cup boiling water, approximately

Toast ground almonds on oven tray in moderate oven 5 minutes or until lightly browned, cool; toast almond kernels in the same way.

Melt butter and chocolate over hot water, stir in sugar, water, egg and sour cream, then sifted flours and ground almonds. Spread into greased base-lined 23cm recess flan tin. Bake in moderate oven 30 to 35 minutes, turn onto wire rack to cool. Spread recess with Mocha Buttercream, refrigerate 1 hour. Cut cake into 16 wedges. Stand wedges on wire rack with a tray underneath. Pour Chocolate Glaze over segments with almonds on top or chocolate dip almonds and use remaining chocolate to drizzle over Mocha Buttercream, allow to set at room temperature, if possible.

Mocha Buttercream: Melt chocolate over hot water. Beat egg yolks in small bowl with electric mixer until pale and thick. Combine sugar and water in pan, stir over heat without boiling until sugar is dissolved. Increase heat, boil without stirring for 7 minutes or until syrup is slightly thickened (106°C on a sweets thermometer). Gradually add syrup in a thin stream to egg yolks, while beating, beat until mixture cools. Cream butter in small bowl with electric mixer, beat in egg yolk mixture, cooled chocolate and combined coffee and water.

Chocolate Glaze: Melt chocolate and butter over hot water. Beat in icing sugar and enough boiling water to give a thick pouring consistency.

■ **TO FREEZE:** Cooled uniced cake can be frozen for up to a month.
Note: This recipe is not suitable to microwave.

LEMON ALMOND TART

Lemon Butter can be made at least 2 weeks in advance; keep refrigerated. Tart can be made 2 days in advance; store covered in refrigerator. We used a small amount of commercially made lemon butter to pipe onto the tart.

PASTRY
1 cup plain flour
2 tablespoons castor sugar
60g butter
2 egg yolks
1 tablespoon water, approximately

LEMON BUTTER
60g butter
⅓ cup sugar
¼ cup lemon juice
2 egg yolks

FILLING
90g butter
1 teaspoon vanilla
½ cup castor sugar
1 cup (125g) ground almonds
2 eggs, lightly beaten

Pastry: Sift flour into bowl, add sugar, rub in butter. Add egg yolks and enough water to mix to a firm dough. Roll out on floured surface large enough to line 23cm flan tin. Bake blind by covering pastry with greaseproof paper and sprinkling thickly with rice or beans. Bake in moderately hot oven 10 minutes. Remove paper and beans, return pastry case to oven for 5 minutes; cool slightly. Spread Lemon Butter over base, top with Filling, bake in moderate oven 30 minutes or until set. Cool, decorate with whipped cream and toasted flaked almonds, if desired.

Lemon Butter: Combine butter, sugar, lemon juice and egg yolks in bowl or in top of double saucepan, stir over simmering water until mixture thickens slightly; cool.

Filling: Cream butter, vanilla and sugar in small bowl with electric mixer; stir in almonds and eggs.

■ **TO FREEZE:** Cool tart, wrap securely, freeze for up to 2 months. Thaw at room temperature for several hours before serving.

Note: This recipe is not suitable to microwave.

Above right: Almond Chocolate Wedges.
Right: Lemon Almond Tart.
Opposite Page: Walnut and Orange Gateau.
Plate, above right, is Tempo Eighty Axis from Mikasa and tiles are Gabrinelli Pink from Fred Pazotti; Italian platter, right, is from Saywell Imports and tiles are Handbrush Grey from Fred Pazotti; glass plates, opposite page, are from Mikasa.

SUPER RICH CHOCOLATE FUDGE

Store fudge in refrigerator for up to a month, if desired.

125g butter
1½ cups castor sugar
⅔ cup canned evaporated milk
100g packet white marshmallows
185g dark chocolate, chopped
1 teaspoon vanilla

Combine butter, sugar, milk and marshmallows in heavy based pan. Stir over heat without boiling until sugar is dissolved and marshmallows melted, then boil 8 minutes stirring constantly (mixture should reach 102°C on a sweets thermometer). Remove from heat, stir in chocolate and vanilla, beat until chocolate is melted and mixture begins to thicken.

Spead mixture quickly into bar tin (base measures 7cm x 25cm) which has been lined with greased foil. Refrigerate for several hours before cutting the fudge into squares.

■ **TO MICROWAVE:** Combine butter, sugar, milk and marshmallows in medium bowl, cook on MEDIUM HIGH 5 minutes, stirring occasionally to dissolve sugar and melt butter. Cook on MEDIUM HIGH 10 minutes without stirring. Stir in vanilla, then chocolate piece by piece; continue as above.

Note: This recipe is not suitable to freeze.

PISTACHIO BREAD

This bread can be kept in an airtight container for at least a month providing the sliced bread has been dried out correctly in the oven.

3 egg whites
½ cup castor sugar
1 cup plain flour, sifted
250g pistachio nuts, shelled

Beat egg whites in small basin with electric mixer until soft peaks form, add sugar gradually, beat until dissolved. Fold in flour and pistachio nuts. Spread mixture into greased bar tin (base measures 7cm x 25 cm). Bake in moderate oven 30 minutes or until light golden brown. Turn onto wire rack to cool, when cold wrap in foil. Stand 1 or 2 days, then slice thinly using a very sharp knife or electric knife. Place slices in single layer onto oven trays, bake in slow oven 45 minutes or until dry and crisp.

Note: This recipe is not suitable to freeze or microwave.

CREAMY PRALINE CHOCOLATE CASES

Foil chocolate cases are available from gourmet shops and specialty kitchenware stores. The cheaper compound cooking chocolate will maintain a good shape and gloss at room temperature. Chocolate cases and praline can be made up to 2 days before required, if desired. Add cream filling up to 3 hours before serving.

125g compound dark chocolate, chopped
½ cup castor sugar
⅓ cup slivered almonds
300ml carton thickened cream

Melt chocolate over hot water, use a teaspoon to coat the insides of 24 foil cases, refrigerate until set. Peel away cases from chocolate.

Place sugar in heavy pan, place over medium heat until sugar begins to melt; do not stir. When sugar starts to brown, stir gently to dissolve remaining sugar. Spread almonds onto lightly greased oven tray, pour hot syrup evenly over almonds.

When set, break into pieces, then chop finely. Whip cream until soft peaks form, fold in half the almond praline, spoon into chocolate cases. Sprinkle with remaining almond praline, refrigerate until ready to serve.

Note: This recipe is not suitable to freeze.

Makes about 24.

CHOCOLATE ORANGE TRUFFLES

Truffles will keep well in refrigerator, covered, for up to a month.

200g white chocolate, chopped
60g unsalted butter
¼ cup cream
¼ cup icing sugar, sifted
1 tablespoon Grand Marnier
1 teaspoon grated orange rind
200g dark chocolate, chopped

Melt white chocolate and butter over hot water. Stir in cream, icing sugar, Grand Marnier and orange rind. Refrigerate mixture covered for several hours or until firm. Shape mixture into 2cm balls, refrigerate 1 hour. Melt dark chocolate over hot water; using 2 teaspoons coat balls in chocolate. Refrigerate on foil-covered tray until set.

■ **TO MICROWAVE:** Combine white chocolate and butter in bowl, cook on HIGH 2 minutes stirring once. Proceed as above. Place dark chocolate in bowl, cook on HIGH 2 minutes stirring once. Proceed as above.

Note: This recipe is not suitable to freeze.

Makes about 20.

SESAME BRITTLE

Brittle can be made and stored in airtight container at room temperature for up to 2 weeks.

2 tablespoons sesame seeds
2 cups sugar
¾ cup water
2 tablespoons golden syrup
60g butter
½ teaspoon bicarbonate of soda

Place sesame seeds in pan, stir constantly over heat until lightly browned; cool. Grease and line a 23cm square tin with foil, extending foil over sides of tin. Combine sugar and water in pan, stir over heat without boiling until sugar has dissolved. Increase heat, boil without stirring until golden brown, about 15 minutes; test by dropping a teaspoonful of mixture into a cup of cold water; it will set to a hard crack when it is ready. Add golden syrup and butter, stir gently over heat until just combined. Gently stir in sesame seeds and soda. Pour into tin, stand about 5 minutes or until nearly set, lift out of tin, mark into squares with knife, cutting nearly all the way through. When set, cut or break into squares.

■ **TO MICROWAVE:** Combine sugar and water in deep 2 litre dish, cook on HIGH 5 minutes or until sugar has dissolved, stirring occasionally. Cook on HIGH further 10 minutes or until golden brown; continue as above.

Note: This recipe is not suitable to freeze.

In descending order: Super Rich Chocolate Fudge with Sesame Brittle; Pistachio Bread; Chocolate Orange Truffles with Creamy Praline Chocolate Cases.
Glass bowl is Scala from Orrefors, china is Tempo Eighty Tatami Peach from Mikasa and the Italian white tray is from Saywell Imports.

TRADITIONAL CHRISTMAS DINNER FOR 10

TURKEY WITH HAM AND APRICOT SEASONING

SWEET POTATOES WITH BRANDIED MARMALADE GLAZE

STIR-FRIED SNOW PEAS WITH MUSHROOMS

BROCCOLI AND CAULIFLOWER IN SOUR CREAM SAUCE

CRISPY PARMESAN POTATOES

STEAMED APRICOT PUDDING WITH CREAMY BRANDY SAUCE

FRUIT MINCE TARTLETS

Most families gather together for Christmas dinner. The meal we have planned for you is traditional but updated to cater for all generations and tastes.

TURKEY WITH HAM AND APRICOT SEASONING

4kg turkey
4 bacon rashers
30g butter, melted
½ cup water
HAM AND APRICOT SEASONING
30g butter
1 onion, chopped
1 clove garlic, crushed
1 stick celery, chopped
¼ cup finely chopped dried apricots
2 cups stale breadcrumbs
500g ham, minced
½ cup chopped parsley
1 egg, lightly beaten
½ teaspoon mixed herbs
SAUCE
4 cups water
few whole peppercorns
1 onion, sliced
¼ cup plain flour
2 teaspoons redcurrant jelly
2 tablespoons port

STEP 1
Remove neck and giblets from inside turkey, reserve for Sauce. Rinse turkey, pat dry inside and out. Tuck wings under body.

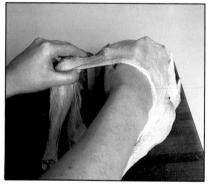

STEP 2
Carefully loosen skin over breast and top of legs, using fingers or the handle of a wooden spoon.

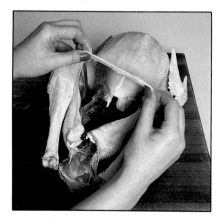

STEP 3
Cut bacon into 8cm lengths, push bacon under skin of turkey over breast and legs.

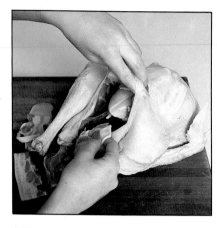

STEP 4
Fill cavity of turkey loosely with Ham and Apricot Seasoning, tie legs together, brush turkey with butter.

Place a wire rack in a baking dish, add water to dish, place turkey on rack. Bake in moderate oven 2½ hours or until turkey is tender. Cover breast and legs of turkey with foil after 1 hour of cooking so that skin does not darken too much. While turkey is cooking, begin to prepare Sauce.

Combine neck and giblets in pan with water, peppercorns and onion. Bring to boil, reduce heat, simmer covered 1 hour; strain, reserve 2½ cups stock for Sauce. Remove turkey from dish, place on oven tray, cover with foil, keep warm while preparing Sauce.

Sauce: Drain fat from pan, leaving about 2 tablespoons of fat in pan, add flour to pan, stir constantly over heat until starting to brown. Gradually stir in reserved stock, redcurrant jelly and port. Stir until Sauce boils and thickens, strain, serve hot over turkey.

Ham and Apricot Seasoning: Melt butter in pan, add onion, garlic and celery, saute few minutes. Stir in remaining ingredients.

Note: This recipe is not suitable to freeze or microwave.

SEASONINGS FOR TURKEY

Here is a selection of delicious seasonings for the Christmas turkey, choose flavors to suit your taste.

SIMPLE HERB SEASONING
60g butter
1 medium onion, finely chopped
2 teaspoons grated lemon rind
2 teaspoons mixed herbs
⅓ cup chopped parsley
4 cups stale breadcrumbs
1 egg, lightly beaten
Heat butter in pan, add onion, saute until onion is soft. Stir in lemon rind, herbs, parsley and breadcrumbs, then egg, mix well.

ROSEMARY AND BACON SEASONING
5 bacon rashers, chopped
2 onions, finely chopped
1 teaspoon dried rosemary leaves
2 sticks celery, finely chopped
125g mushrooms, sliced
4 cups stale breadcrumbs
Add bacon to hot pan, cook stirring until golden brown, remove from pan. Add onions to pan drippings, saute until onions are transparent. Add rosemary, celery and mushrooms, saute for 1 minute, remove from heat, stir in breadcrumbs and bacon.

WHOLEMEAL, CARROT AND WALNUT SEASONING
3 bacon rashers, chopped
6 shallots, chopped
⅓ cup chopped walnuts
1 small carrot, grated
2 teaspoons grated orange rind
½ cup sultanas
4 cups stale wholemeal breadcrumbs
Add bacon to hot pan, cook, stirring, until golden brown, remove from heat. Stir in shallots, walnuts, carrot, orange rind and sultanas, mix in breadcrumbs.

CURRIED RICE AND APPLE SEASONING
4 bacon rashers, chopped
1 onion, finely chopped
2 teaspoons curry powder
2½ cups cooked rice
1 cup stale breadcrumbs
⅓ cup chopped dried apples
Saute bacon, onion and curry powder in pan until onion is tender, mix into combined rice and breadcrumbs. Cook apples in boiling water for 1 minute until slightly softened, drain, stir through rice mixture.

SWEET POTATOES WITH BRANDIED MARMALADE GLAZE

This dish can be prepared up to a day ahead of time. Cover partly cooked potatoes with glaze, keep covered in refrigerator until cooking time. Use the colorful kumara or the white sweet potatoes; either gives a delicious result. We used the slightly bitter Seville orange marmalade for this recipe.

1kg sweet potatoes, thickly sliced
BRANDIED MARMALADE GLAZE
½ cup orange marmalade
½ cup orange juice
2 teaspoons grated fresh ginger
1 teaspoon french mustard
15g butter
1 tablespoon brandy

China is Spode Christmas Tree from Shorters; glasses are Orrefors Claire.

Boil or steam potatoes for 5 minutes or until partly cooked. Drain, place potatoes in lightly greased shallow ovenproof dish in single layer. Top with Glaze, bake uncovered in moderate oven for 30 minutes.

Brandied Marmalade Glaze: Combine marmalade, juice, ginger and mustard in pan. Simmer uncovered for 10 minutes or until slightly reduced. Remove from heat, stir in butter and brandy.

■ **TO MICROWAVE:** Place potatoes in dish with 2 tablespoons of water, cook covered on HIGH 5 minutes, drain, top with Glaze, cook on HIGH 5 minutes or until potatoes are tender.

Brandied Marmalade Glaze: Reduce orange juice to ¼ cup, combine all ingredients in bowl except brandy, cook on HIGH 2 minutes, add brandy.

Note: This recipe is not suitable to freeze.

STIR-FRIED SNOW PEAS WITH MUSHROOMS

1 tablespoon oil
1 clove garlic, crushed
250g baby mushrooms
250g snow peas, topped, tailed
1 tablespoon light soy sauce
½ × 230g can water chestnuts, drained, sliced

Heat oil and garlic in large pan or wok, add mushrooms, stir-fry 1 minute. Add snow peas, stir-fry one minute. Add soy sauce and water chestnuts, stir-fry 1 minute. Serve immediately.

■ **TO MICROWAVE:** Combine oil, garlic and mushrooms in large bowl, cook on HIGH 3 minutes, add snow peas, soy sauce and water chestnuts, cover, cook on HIGH 3 minutes or until snow peas are just tender.

Note: This recipe is not suitable to freeze.

BROCCOLI AND CAULIFLOWER IN SOUR CREAM SAUCE

This recipe can be prepared the day before required, covered and refrigerated until ready to cook.

500g broccoli
1 small (1kg) cauliflower
SAUCE
90g butter
2 onions, finely chopped
2 tablespoons plain flour
2 tablespoons brown sugar
1 teaspoon dry mustard
1½ cups milk
1 cup sour cream
2 tablespoons chopped parsley

Cut broccoli and cauliflower into flowerets. Boil or steam broccoli and cauliflower until just tender; drain. Place into heatproof serving dish, pour Sauce over, serve immediately; or, if necessary to reheat, cover, bake in moderate oven 20 minutes.
Sauce: Melt butter in pan, add onion, saute until onion is soft. Add flour, sugar and mustard, stir over heat 1 minute. Gradually stir in milk and sour cream, stir over heat until Sauce boils and thickens; add parsley.

■ **TO MICROWAVE:** Place broccoli and cauliflower in shallow dish in single layer. Add ¼ cup water, cover, cook on HIGH 10 minutes or until vegetables are just tender.
Sauce: Combine butter and onion in bowl, cook on HIGH 5 minutes or until onion is tender. Add flour, sugar and mustard, cook on HIGH 1 minute. Add milk and sour cream, cook on HIGH 3 minutes or until mixture boils and thickens; add parsley. Assemble as above, cover, cook on HIGH 8 minutes or until heated through.
■ **TO FREEZE:** Complete recipe in ovenproof dish, cool, cover, freeze for up to 2 weeks. Reheat in moderate oven while frozen, covered with foil, for 45 minutes or until heated through.

CRISPY PARMESAN POTATOES

Prepare potatoes, place in dish, brush with oil up to 2 hours before baking.

10 medium potatoes
½ cup oil
¼ cup grated parmesan cheese

Peel potatoes, trim to a smooth, rounded shape. Cut a thin slice from base of each potato so they will sit flat. Using a sharp knife, carefully make cuts about 3mm apart from top nearly through to base. Place flat side down in baking dish, brush well with oil, bake in moderate oven 40 minutes, brush occasionally with oil during cooking time. Sprinkle with parmesan cheese, bake further 20 minutes until potatoes are crisp outside and tender inside. Do not turn potatoes during baking.
Note: This recipe is not suitable to freeze or microwave.

STEAMED APRICOT PUDDING
500g dried apricots, chopped
½ cup slivered almonds
⅓ cup halved red glace cherries
1⅓ cups (250g) mixed peel
1 Granny Smith apple, peeled,
grated
½ cup brandy
250g butter
1½ cups brown sugar, firmly packed
4 eggs
1½ cups plain flour, sifted
250g stale white breadcrumbs
(about 4 cups)

Toast almonds on oven tray in moderate oven for 5 minutes, combine in large bowl with apricots, cherries, peel, apple and brandy, mix well.

Have butter and eggs at room temperature. Cream butter and sugar in small bowl with electric mixer; add eggs one at a time, beating between additions, beat only until combined. Add to fruit mixture with flour and breadcrumbs, mix well. Place in well greased steamer (2-litre capacity), cover with foil, place lid on, seal with clips. Bunch remaining foil around edge of steamer to form a tight seal. Place in a large boiler with enough boiling water to come halfway up side of steamer. Boil constantly for 4 hours. Replenish water with boiling water as it evaporates. Serve pudding with Creamy Brandy Sauce or icecream. If not using immediately, leave pudding in steamer. Refrigerate when cold for up to 6 weeks, if desired. When ready to serve steam as above for 2 hours to reheat before serving.
■ **TO FREEZE:** Freeze wrapped in freezer wrap for up to 2 months. Thaw before reheating as above.
Note: This recipe is not suitable to microwave.

CREAMY BRANDY SAUCE
1 cup vanilla icecream
2 teaspoons cornflour
2 teaspoons water
300ml carton thickened cream,
whipped
2 tablespoons icing sugar, sifted
2 tablespoons brandy
Melt icecream in pan over low heat, stir in blended cornflour and water, stir until mixture boils and thickens. Remove from heat, fold in cream, icing sugar and brandy. Serve warm.
■ **TO MICROWAVE:** Place icecream in bowl, cook on HIGH 2 minutes. Proceed as above.
Note: This recipe is not suitable to freeze.

FRUIT MINCE TARTLETS

There is enough pastry to make about 25 tartlets, leftover mince can be stored covered in the refrigerator. It will keep for months. Choose between making your own fruit mince or using the commercial bottled mince and adding more ingredients to make it extra special. Tartlets can be kept, in an airtight container at room temperature for up to 2 weeks.

PASTRY
1½ cups plain flour
125g butter
2 tablespoons castor sugar
1 egg yolk
1 tablespoon water, approximately
Pastry: Sift flour into bowl, rub in butter, add egg yolk, sugar and enough water to mix to a firm dough. Knead on lightly floured surface until smooth, cover, refrigerate 30 minutes. Roll Pastry between two sheets of plastic food wrap to about 2.5mm thickness. Cut out rounds with fluted pastry cutter large enough to line patty pans; fill with Fruit Mince. Bake in moderately hot oven 10 minutes or until lightly browned, cool in tins. Serve topped with whipped cream, if desired.

HOMEMADE FRUIT MINCE
½ cup sultanas
½ cup currants
½ cup finely chopped dates
½ cup finely chopped prunes
½ cup chopped pecan nuts
¼ cup mixed peel
½ cup finely chopped glace apricots
1 small Granny Smith apple, peeled, grated
1 teaspoon finely grated orange rind
¼ cup orange juice
¼ cup Grand Marnier or brandy
¼ cup honey
½ teaspoon mixed spice
QUICK BRANDIED FRUIT MINCE
410g jar fruit mince
1 cup sultanas
1 small Granny Smith apple, peeled, grated
½ cup stale breadcrumbs
1 tablespoon finely chopped glace ginger
2 tablespoons brandy
½ teaspoon mixed spice

Homemade Fruit Mince and Quick Brandied Fruit Mince: Combine all ingredients in large screwtop jar, turn jar daily for 7 days. Mince is now ready to use or can be stored.

■ **TO FREEZE:** Baked tartlets can be cooled, packaged in an airtight container and frozen for up to 2 months. To use, let tartlets come to room temperature.

Note: This recipe is not suitable to microwave.

Here is an American-style wedding cake which has been decorated in a simple but effective way. The cake is always cut by the bride and bridegroom to mark the end of the meal and formalities. It is an indication to let the party begin. Recipes for our Wedding Breakfast begin on page 74. They offer choices to suit the style of wedding and the season.

WEDDING BREAKFAST FOR 50

Cakes can be made up to six months before the wedding, if desired, provided they are stored correctly (see below). Cake can be completely decorated up to two days before the wedding, if desired. Cake boards can be bought already covered from shops which sell cake decorating equipment or make your own from pressed hardboard, then cover with paper. It is correct that this cake recipe does not include self-raising flour or any other raising agent.

AUSTRALIAN WOMEN'S WEEKLY FRUIT CAKE

1¼ kg sultanas
500g raisins, chopped
250g currants
250g mixed peel
250g glace cherries, quartered
⅓ cup marmalade
1 cup rum, brandy, whisky or sherry
500g butter
2 teaspoons grated orange rind
2 teaspoons grated lemon rind
2 cups brown sugar, firmly packed
8 eggs
4 cups plain flour
⅓ cup rum, brandy, whisky or sherry, extra
2 teaspoons mixed spice

To prepare tins: Line base and sides of 2 deep 25cm and 15cm square (or deep 28cm and 18cm round) cake tins with 3 sheets heavy greaseproof paper. The paper should extend 5cm above edges of tins to protect the surface of the cakes during the long cooking time.

Have butter and eggs at room temperature. Combine all fruit, marmalade and rum in large bowl; mix well.

Cream butter and rinds in large bowl with electric mixer until just smooth, add sugar, beat until just combined. Add eggs 1 at a time, beat only until ingredients are combined between additions. The faster the eggs are added the less likely the mixture is to curdle. Add creamed mixture to fruit mixture, mix with hand or wooden spoon until combined. Mix in sifted dry ingredients thoroughly.

Divide mixture between prepared tins, level mixture as evenly as possible. Make the depth of the cake mixture in the smaller tin 5mm less than the depth of the cake mixture in the larger tin. The smaller cake will expand slightly more than the larger cake during cooking. When they are cooked they should be about the same depth — this minimises trimming the cake.

Bake cakes in slow oven, the smaller cake 2 to 2½ hours, the larger cake 3 to 3½ hours. Cakes can be baked on the same shelf of the oven provided tins do not touch each other, the walls of the oven or the door when it is closed. Cakes can also be baked on 2 shelf positions; simply change positions of cakes halfway through the cooking time of the smaller cake.

If it is inconvenient to cook cakes after they are mixed they can be kept covered in the refrigerator for up to 4 weeks. Allow cakes to return to room temperature before baking to simplify estimating cooking time. Cold cakes will take longer to cook.

To test if cakes are cooked, first touch the surface of the centre of the cake with fingertips after minimum given cooking time. If cake feels firm, then use a sharp pointed knife — a vegetable knife is ideal — and push the knife gently right through the centre of the cake, down to the base of the tin. Withdraw the knife gently, feel the blade; it should not feel sticky and should be free of cake mixture. The smaller cake will be lighter in color than the larger cake; it is the longer cooking time that darkens the cake. Also, the cakes will darken more as they cool.

Tear away any lining paper above the edges of the tins, brush the top of the cakes evenly with extra rum. Cover the top of the tins tightly with aluminium foil, then invert tins onto a bench. The cakes will fall out of the tins and flatten as they cool. This also minimises trimming. Cover the tins with a towel to slow down cooling.

Next day, remove the cold cakes from the tins, leave the lining paper intact on the cakes. Wrap the cakes tightly in plastic food wrap, then wrap in foil or teatowels. Store in cool dark place for up to 6 months, if desired. If weather is wet or humid, store cakes in refrigerator. Cakes can be frozen for up to 6 months but there is little point; they will keep perfectly in the refrigerator or at a cool room temperature.
Note: This recipe is not suitable to microwave.

TO DECORATE CAKE

Remove lining paper carefully from cakes, invert cakes onto pieces of greaseproof paper. Trim cakes if necessary so they will sit flat and be of the same height.
You will need:
1½kg packaged almond or marzipan paste
1kg packaged white soft icing
500g pure icing sugar, sifted
2 egg whites, lightly beaten
33cm covered square board
15cm covered square board
fine wire — florists' or cake decorators'
tapers or fine candles
artificial daisies
ribbon for loops and knife

STEP 1

Work packets of almond paste together until smooth and pliable. Use only enough icing sugar to prevent paste sticking to bench. Work in icing sugar only if almond paste is sticky. Brush large cake evenly and fairly heavily with egg white. Cut off ⅔ of the paste, wrap remaining paste in plastic to keep airtight. Roll paste out on bench dusted with icing sugar, roll out paste evenly, large enough to cover base and sides of cake.

Lift paste onto cake with the help of the rolling pin, then lightly and carefully mould paste onto cake with sugared hands; trim edges neatly. Leave cake to stand at room temperature for at least 6 hours or until the paste has developed a slight crust. Do not leave cake more than a day or two or paste will dry out too much. Cover small cake in the same way.

STEP 2

Knead packets of soft icing together with a little icing sugar until smooth and icing loses its stickiness. Roll out $\frac{1}{3}$ of the icing to a square large enough to cover the top of the small cake. Brush top of cake lightly but evenly with a little egg white, then lift icing onto cake. Smooth with sugared hands until icing extends over sides of cake by about 1cm. Cut off excess icing close to sides of cake, smooth rough edges with sugared fingers. Place cakes on covered boards.

Use 4 butchers' wooden skewers to support the small cake. Push skewers into large cake, point side first. Remove skewers, push skewers into cake blunt side first. Mark skewers level with the top of the cake, cut off skewers with serrated knife. Push skewers back into cake, as shown. Measure and cut skewers one at a time, so they are returned to their original position in the cake. Place small cake on top of large cake.

STEP 3
FLUFFY FROSTING
1 cup sugar
$\frac{1}{3}$ cup water
2 egg whites

Combine sugar and water in small pan, stir over heat without boiling until sugar is dissolved. Brush any sugar grains down from side of saucepan with brush dipped in water. Increase heat, boil rapidly without stirring uncovered for 3 to 5 minutes. If a sweets thermometer is available, syrup should reach 115 degrees C. Otherwise you can test by dropping 1 teaspoon of syrup into cold water; it should form a ball of soft sticky toffee when rolled between fingers. If testing syrup in water, remove pan from heat when syrup falls from spoon in a heavy drop, allow bubbles to subside, then test in cold water. The syrup should not change color; if it does, it has been cooked for too long and you will have to throw out that batch and start again.

While syrup is boiling, beat egg whites in small bowl with electric mixer until stiff, keep beating (or whites will deflate) while syrup is reaching the correct temperature. When syrup is ready, allow bubbles to subside, pour in a very thin stream onto the egg whites while they are beating on medium speed, as shown. If syrup is added too quickly, Frosting will not thicken. Continue beating and adding syrup until all syrup is used. Continue to beat until Frosting will stand in stiff peaks; Frosting should be warm at this stage.

STEP 4

Spread Frosting over sides of cakes, as shown. Be sure to cover board of top tier and extend Frosting down enough to form a seal. The cake can be easily removed for cutting by sliding spatula under board of small cake.

STEP 5

Decorate with artificial flowers, loops of ribbon wired securely and tapers. With a skewer pierce holes in cake in which to position flowers and ribbon loops.

Storage of top tier of wedding cake: Place cake in cardboard box, seal securely to eliminate dust, store in cool dark place. Check cake during wet or humid weather. If it looks sticky, buy some silica gel from the chemist and sprinkle the crystals around the cake; these will absorb the excess moisture from the air trapped in the sealed box. The icing might deteriorate during this time, but the almond paste, provided it has been used correctly, will preserve the cake for some months.

All of these savories can be made a day before required, if desired, and kept covered in the refrigerator ready to cook or serve. The savories take the place of the first course in this menu for 50. We suggest you make all of these recipes for variety in flavor, texture and color.

CHEESE AND BACON SAVORIES

Savories can be prepared and refrigerated, covered, 24 hours before baking and serving.

2 bacon rashers, finely chopped
1 cup grated tasty cheese
2 olives, chopped
2 tablespoons mayonnaise
1 tablespoon drained canned diced capsicum
1 tablespoon chopped parsley
3 green shallots, chopped
¼ teaspoon curry powder
14 slices white bread
30g butter, melted

Cook bacon in pan until crisp; drain bacon on absorbent paper. Combine bacon, cheese, olives, mayonnaise, capsicum, parsley, shallots and curry powder, mix well. Remove crusts from bread, flatten bread with rolling pin, spread a layer of cheese mixture over bread, roll up, secure with toothpick. Place savories on oven tray, brush with butter, bake in moderate oven 10 minutes or until golden brown.

Makes 28.

■ **TO FREEZE:** Freeze on tray, then pack in airtight container. Freeze for up to 2 months. To use, place frozen savories on greased oven tray, bake in slow oven 20 minutes.

Note: This recipe is not suitable to microwave.

CHEESE 'N' CHIVE STUFFED TOMATOES

Tomatoes can be prepared and refrigerated, covered, up to 24 hours.

⅓ cup slivered almonds, chopped
2 x 250g punnets cherry tomatoes
125g packet cream cheese, softened
1 small red pepper, finely chopped
2 tablespoons finely chopped chives

Toast almonds on oven tray in moderate oven for about 5 minutes. Slice top from each tomato, scoop out seeds, reserve 2 tablespoons pulp and add to filling. Beat cream cheese until smooth, stir in almonds, red pepper, chives and reserved tomato pulp. Place filling into tomatoes, refrigerate 1 hour or until firm.

Makes about 25.

Note: This recipe is not suitable to freeze.

CREAMY SALMON DILL PINWHEELS

Prepare these rolls up to a day before serving, if desired. Keep covered in refrigerator. Slice just before serving.

WHOLEMEAL CREPES
3 eggs
½ cup wholemeal self-raising flour
½ cup wholemeal plain flour
¾ cup milk
¾ cup water

SALMON DILL FILLING
440g can red salmon, drained
250g butter, softened
1 teaspoon grated lemon rind
¼ cup lemon juice
2 tablespoons chopped dill (or 1 teaspoon dried dill tips)

Wholemeal Crepes: Sift flours into bowl, make well in centre of dry ingredients; gradually stir in lightly beaten eggs, milk and water. Refrigerate 1 hour. Heat lightly oiled pan. Pour about 2 or 3 tablespoons of mixture from a

jug into pan. Cook until mixture is set and golden brown underneath. Turn crepe, cook on other side. Repeat with remaining batter. This recipe makes about 16 Crepes.

Spread cold Crepes with Filling. Stack one Crepe on top of another and roll the two Crepes together like a swiss roll. Repeat with remaining Crepes. Refrigerate until firm enough to slice. Trim ends from rolls, cut into 1cm slices.

Salmon Dill Filling: Remove bones from salmon. Beat butter in small bowl with electric mixer until creamy, beat in salmon, lemon rind, juice and dill.

■**TO FREEZE:** Place rolls on tray, freeze until firm, wrap, store in airtight container for up to 2 weeks. To use, slice rolls while firm, allow to come to room temperature before using.

Note: This recipe is not suitable to microwave.

Makes about 48.

On plate at left: Cheese 'n' Chive Stuffed Tomatoes; Creamy Salmon Dill Pinwheels; Curried Egg Butter on Pumpernickel. On plate at right: Mushroom Pate Triangles; Cheese and Bacon Savories. China is Wedgwood Coalport Countryware; glasses are Mikasa Wheaton.

MUSHROOM PATE TRIANGLES

We used a Grand Marnier pate bought from a delicatessen; buy the best pate you can or make your own. The triangles can be prepared up to 12 hours before cooking, if desired. Keep covered in refrigerator. To fold pastry in triangles, see photograph at left.

7 sheets fillo pastry
30g butter
250g baby mushrooms, sliced
250g pate
1⅓ cup, packaged breadcrumbs
½ cup sour cream
2 eggs, lightly beaten
2 tablespoons chopped parsley
125g butter, extra

Heat butter in pan, add mushrooms, cook stirring until soft. Place mushrooms into bowl, stir in pate, breadcrumbs, sour cream, egg and parsley. Brush one sheet of fillo pastry at a time with extra butter (cover remaining sheets with a piece of greaseproof paper, then a damp cloth); cut pastry lengthwise into 4 long strips. Brush each strip with extra melted butter, fold in half, brush with butter, place a heaped teaspoonful of mushroom mixture onto each end, fold up into a triangle, brush with more melted butter. Place triangles on ungreased oven trays, bake in moderately hot oven 10 minutes or until golden brown and crisp. Repeat with remaining pastry and filling.

Makes about 28.

■**TO FREEZE:** Freeze unbaked triangles on tray, then seal in airtight container. Freeze for up to 2 months. Thaw before baking, as above.

Note: This recipe is not suitable to microwave.

CURRIED EGG BUTTER ON PUMPERNICKEL

Egg Butter can be made one day before required: keep covered and refrigerated. Pipe onto pumpernickel up to 2 hours beforehand, if desired, cover, refrigerate.

125g butter, softened
60g packaged cream cheese, softened
2 tablespoons chutney
2 teaspoons curry powder
1 onion, chopped
8 hard-boiled eggs, chopped
250g packet pumpernickel rounds
red and black caviar

Blend or process butter, cream cheese, chutney, curry and onion until smooth. Add eggs, blend until smooth, refrigerate until firm. Pipe mixture onto pumpernickel rounds. When ready to serve, garnish with caviar.

Makes 20.

Note: This recipe is not suitable to freeze.

MAIN COURSES

CREAMY ZUCCHINI WITH SEAFOOD

CURRIED CHICKEN AND ONIONS BENEDICTINE

MINTED LAMB IN RED WINE

PORK FILLET WITH TANGY PLUM SAUCE

VEAL PAPRIKA WITH SOUR CREAM

ACCOMPANIMENTS

GREEN AND WHITE TAGLIATELLE

PEPPERED POTATOES AND CARROTS IN SOUR CREAM

TASTY GARLIC VEGETABLES

APRICOT AND CHESTNUT RICE

BABY SQUASH WITH BACON

It is difficult to estimate how much food your guests will eat so we have leaned toward being generous. A lot depends on the age of the guests, the time of day or night and, of course, the season — most people eat more on a cold winter's night. If the wedding is to be held in summer, you might prefer to drop one or two of the hot main courses and serve cold meat dishes, and also drop two or three of the accompaniments and serve salads instead. See our Summer Party for 30 (page 44) for more ideas.

All of the main courses and accompaniments will serve 10 people when made individually. We don't recommend that you make more than this quantity at the one time. When you are deciding the menu, it is easy to halve these recipes to try them on your family and friends. You might also like to have only three varieties of main courses — in this case simply make two batches of two of the dishes and one batch of one other dish to make the food sufficient to serve 50 people.

CREAMY ZUCCHINI WITH SEAFOOD

Prepare seafood (including poaching scallops) and sauce up to 12 hours before required. Assemble dish as close to reheating and serving time as possible or zucchini will be watery.

2kg cooked prawns, shelled
1kg scallops
24 oysters
1 cup water
1 cup dry white wine
300ml carton cream
1 clove garlic, crushed
1 tablespoon cornflour
1 tablespoon lemon juice
pinch saffron powder
2 tablespoons grated parmesan cheese
30g butter
500g zucchini, grated

Bring water and wine to boil in pan, add scallops, return to boil; drain, reserve liquid. Return liquid to pan, add cream and garlic, boil uncovered until reduced by half. Add blended cornflour and lemon juice, stir until sauce boils and thickens, reduce heat, simmer 10 minutes. Stir in tiny pinch saffron (to color sauce slightly) and cheese. Melt butter in pan, add zucchini, cook over high heat 1 minute or until just soft. Stir zucchini and seafood into sauce, stir until heated through.
Note: This recipe is not suitable to freeze or microwave.

GREEN AND WHITE TAGLIATELLE

Cooking time of tagliatelle will depend on whether fresh or packaged pasta is used; somewhere between 3 and 12 minutes is a guide.

500g green tagliatelle
500g white tagliatelle
SAUCE
185g butter
1 teaspoon grated lemon rind
1 tablespoon lemon juice
1 clove garlic, crushed
¼ cup grated parmesan cheese

Below: Creamy Zucchini with Seafood; Green and White Tagliatelle.

Drop tagliatelle into pan of boiling water, boil rapidly uncovered until just tender, drain. Pour Sauce over pasta, toss lightly.

Sauce: Combine butter, rind, juice, garlic and cheese in pan, stir over low heat until butter is melted.

Note: This recipe is not suitable to freeze or microwave.

CURRIED CHICKEN AND ONIONS BENEDICTINE

This dish can be cooked completely up to 2 days ahead, if desired; store covered in refrigerator. Benedictine adds a special flavor to this recipe; brandy is a fairly good substitute. We used a mild curry powder; increase quantity if a hotter curry is required.

1½kg (about 10) chicken breast fillets
60g butter
30g butter, extra
3 large onions, sliced
1 tablespoon curry powder
3 cups chicken stock
½ cup Benedictine
⅓ cup plain flour
⅓ cup water
½ cup cream

Cut chicken into strips. Melt butter in large pan, add chicken, stir-fry over high heat until cooked and lightly browned all over, remove from pan. Melt extra butter in pan, add onion, saute until lightly browned, add curry, cook stirring 1 minute. Add combined stock and Benedictine, stir in blended flour and water, add cream. Stir until sauce boils and thickens, reduce heat, simmer until mixture is reduced by one third. Return chicken to sauce, heat through gently just before serving.

Note: This recipe is not suitable to freeze or microwave.

Above: Curried Chicken and Onions Benedictine; Peppered Potatoes and Carrots in Sour Cream.
China is Mikasa Harrow; cutlery is Mikasa Estashi.

PEPPERED POTATOES AND CARROTS IN SOUR CREAM

This dish is easier to prepare if a food processor is used. Use the grater blade for the potatoes and onions, the slicing blade for the carrots and the mixing blade for the cream cheese and sour cream. This dish can be prepared the morning of the wedding and baked later that day.

5 large (800g) potatoes, grated
1 onion, grated
5 medium (500g) carrots, thinly sliced
2 chicken stock cubes
300ml carton sour cream
125g packet cream cheese
2 teaspoons canned green peppercorns, drained
2 tablespoons chopped chives

Place potatoes and onion in large bowl. Blend or process stock cubes, sour cream, cheese and peppercorns, mix into potatoes. Place half the potato mixture into a greased shallow ovenproof dish (2.5-litre capacity). Top with half the carrots, then remaining potato mixture, then remaining carrots. Cover, bake in moderately slow oven 1½ hours or until vegetables are tender. Sprinkle with chives before serving.

■**TO MICROWAVE:** Place potato and onion in shallow dish, cover, cook on HIGH 6 minutes, combine with sour cream mixture. Place carrots in shallow dish, add 1 tablespoon water, cover, cook on HIGH 6 minutes, drain. Layer potatoes and carrots as above, cover, cook on HIGH 6 minutes or until vegetables are tender.

Note: This recipe is not suitable to freeze.

MINTED LAMB IN RED WINE

Ask butcher to bone out legs of lamb for you. This dish can be cooked completely, cooled, covered and refrigerated up to 2 days before serving.

2 × 1½ kg boned out legs of lamb
60g butter
4 onions, chopped
4 bacon rashers, chopped
½ cup plain flour
2 cups red wine
3 cups beef stock
⅓ cup chopped mint (or 1
   tablespoon dried mint)
1 tablespoon mint jelly
¼ cup tomato paste
⅓ cup chopped parsley
2 × 400g cans tomatoes

Cut lamb into bite-sized cubes. Heat butter in pan, add onions, saute until soft, remove from pan; add bacon to pan, cook until crisp, drain on absorbent paper. Add sufficient lamb to hot pan to cover base of pan in single layer, stir constantly over high heat until lamb is browned all over. This is important for good color and flavor. Repeat with remaining lamb. Place onions, bacon and lamb in large ovenproof dish, or in boiler, stir in blended flour and wine, stock, mint, mint jelly, tomato paste, ¼ cup of the parsley, and undrained crushed tomatoes. Cover dish, bake in moderate oven 2½ to 3 hours or until lamb is tender; stir two or three times during cooking. Or, bring to boil stirring, reduce heat, simmer covered 1½ hours or until lamb is tender. Sprinkle with remaining parsley just before serving.

■ **TO FREEZE:** Cool lamb mixture, seal in airtight container, freeze for up to 2 months. Add some more chopped mint and parsley before serving.

Note: This recipe is not suitable to microwave.

TASTY GARLIC VEGETABLES

Prepare vegetables a day before required. Cook as close to serving time as possible for best results.

750g cauliflower
1kg butternut pumpkin
375g green beans
30g butter
1 onion, coarsely chopped
1 chicken stock cube
2 cloves garlic, crushed
¾ cup water
⅓ cup grated parmesan cheese

Cut cauliflower into flowerets, cut pumpkin into chunks about the same size as flowerets. Cut beans in half. Boil or steam cauliflower and pumpkin until just tender. Heat butter in pan, add onion, cook until soft, add crumbled stock cube, garlic and beans, cover, cook for about 3 minutes or until beans are bright green. Add cauliflower and pumpkin, stir-fry 3 minutes. Add water, cover, cook 5 minutes; serve sprinkled with cheese.

Note: This recipe is not suitable to freeze or microwave.

PORK FILLET WITH TANGY PLUM SAUCE

Sauce can be made the day before the wedding and pork marinaded overnight. Cooking is best left as close to serving time as possible.

1kg pork fillet
2 tablespoons oil, approximately
1 clove garlic, crushed
2 red peppers, chopped
2 onions, coarsely chopped
4 sticks celery, coarsely chopped
TANGY PLUM SAUCE
825g can red plums
2 tablespoons grated fresh ginger
¼ cup dry sherry
1 tablespoon soy sauce
1 tablespoon hoi sin sauce
1 tablespoon plum sauce
1 tablespoon honey
½ teaspoon five spice powder

Remove sinew from pork, slice pork thinly, marinade in Tangy Plum Sauce overnight or for at least 1 hour.

Heat oil with garlic in large pan. Add onions, celery and pepper to pan, stir-fry until onions are soft, remove from pan. Add drained pork in several batches, stir-fry pork until well browned all over. If necessary, add a little more oil to the pan during cooking. Return vegetables to pan, add Sauce and pureed plums. Bring Sauce to the boil, cover, reduce heat, simmer few minutes.

Tangy Plum Sauce: Drain plums, reserve 1 cup syrup. Remove stones from plums, puree plums in blender or processor.

Combine reserved syrup, juice squeezed from ginger, sherry, soy sauce, hoi sin sauce, plum sauce, honey and five spice powder in bowl.
Note: This recipe is not suitable to freeze or microwave.

APRICOT AND CHESTNUT RICE

Rice mixture can be prepared a day ahead, cover, refrigerate; omit shallots and parsley until ready to serve.

½ cup finely chopped dried apricots
¼ cup dry white wine
6 cups water
2 chicken stock cubes
1 cup brown rice
1 cup white rice
½ teaspoon turmeric
140g can water chestnuts, drained, chopped
6 green shallots, chopped
¼ cup chopped parsley

Soak apricots in wine while rice is cooking. Bring water and crumbled stock cubes to boil in large pan, add brown rice, boil rapidly uncovered for 20 minutes, add white rice, boil further 10 minutes or until rice is tender. Drain rice, combine with apricot mixture, turmeric, water chestnuts, shallots and parsley; mix well.

■ **TO MICROWAVE:** Omit shallots and parsley. Cooked rice can be reheated covered in a microwave oven on HIGH 5 minutes; toss lightly halfway through reheating time; add shallots and parsley just before serving.

■ **TO FREEZE:** Omit shallots and parsley; prepare recipe as above. Thaw rice, reheat in microwave oven or in lightly greased, covered ovenproof dish in moderate oven for about 20 minutes or until hot. Toss in shallots and parsley just before serving.

Opposite page: Minted Lamb in Red Wine; Tasty Garlic Vegetables.
Below: Pork Fillet with Tangy Plum Sauce; Apricot and Chestnut Rice.

VEAL PAPRIKA WITH SOUR CREAM

If desired, cook veal mixture, cool, cover and refrigerate up to 2 days before serving. Add almonds, sour cream and mushrooms when reheating.

2½ kg stewing veal
60g butter
4 onions, chopped
2 tablespoons paprika
2 cloves garlic, crushed
½ cup plain flour
4 cups beef stock
1 tablespoon french mustard
½ cup chopped parsley
200g slivered almonds
2 × 300ml cartons sour cream
500g baby mushrooms

Cut veal into bite-sized cubes. Heat butter in large pan, add onions, saute until soft, add paprika and garlic, cook stirring a few minutes, transfer to large ovenproof dish or boiler. Reheat pan, add veal gradually to pan in batches in single layer, stir constantly over high heat until veal is browned all over. This will give you a well flavored, well colored, finished dish. Repeat with remaining veal. Add meat to ovenproof dish or boiler with blended flour and stock, mustard and ¼ cup of the chopped parsley, mix well. Cover, bake in moderate oven 2½ to 3 hours or until veal is tender; stir two or three times during cooking. Or, bring to boil, stirring, reduce heat, simmer covered 1½ hours or until veal is tender. Toast almonds on oven tray in moderate oven for 5 minutes. Stir into veal mixture with sour cream and mushrooms, bake further 30 minutes or simmer further 10 minutes. Serve sprinkled with remaining parsley.

■ **TO FREEZE:** Cook veal mixture until tender, cool, seal in airtight container, freeze. Add toasted almonds, sour cream, mushrooms and parsley after reheating and just before serving.
Note: This recipe is not suitable to microwave.

BABY SQUASH WITH BACON

For best flavor and color, cook as close to serving time as possible.

500g green baby squash
500g yellow baby squash
5 bacon rashers, chopped
1 onion, finely chopped
1 clove garlic, crushed
1 small red pepper, chopped
30g butter
1 tablespoon brandy
2 tablespoons chopped chives

Cook bacon in pan with onion, garlic, pepper and butter until bacon is crisp and onion soft. Steam or boil squash until just tender; drain, stir into bacon mixture with brandy and chives.

■ **TO MICROWAVE:** Combine bacon, onion, garlic, pepper and butter in large bowl, cook on HIGH 5 minutes. Place squash in large shallow dish with ¼ cup of water, cover, cook on HIGH 4 minutes or until squash are just tender. Drain, stir in bacon mixture with brandy and chives. Reheat on HIGH 1 minute just before serving.
Note: This recipe is not suitable to freeze.

Veal Paprika with Sour Cream; Baby Squash with Bacon.

All the desserts serve ten when made individually. Make all five varieties for the wedding or, double up on two or three of your favorites. Look at the desserts with our Summer Party for 30 for more luscious ideas.

DESSERTS

CHEESE CRUSTED APPLE PIE

Make Pie completely the day before required, if desired

CHEESE PASTRY
1 cup plain flour
½ cup self-raising flour
2 tablespoons castor sugar
125g butter
½ cup grated tasty cheese
¼ cup water, approximately
FILLING
4 large Granny Smith apples, peeled
1 tablespoon lemon juice
1 tablespoon plain flour
⅓ cup sugar
¼ teaspoon cinnamon
TOPPING
⅓ cup brown sugar
⅓ cup plain flour
½ cup coarsely chopped pecan nuts
60g butter

Cheese Pastry: Sift flours and sugar into bowl, rub in butter, add cheese, then enough water to mix to a firm dough. Press Pastry into a ball, cover, refrigerate 30 minutes.

Roll Pastry large enough to line 23cm flan tin; trim edges. Cover Pastry with a piece of greaseproof paper, cover paper with dried peas, beans or rice, etc. Bake in moderately hot oven 7 minutes, carefully remove paper and beans, bake further 7 minutes, cool. Place Filling into pastry case, sprinkle with Topping. Bake in moderately hot oven 15 minutes, reduce heat to moderate, bake further 15 minutes; cool to room temperature. Decorate with whipped cream, extra chopped pecans and icing sugar, if desired.

Filling: Chop apples coarsely, add to pan with lemon juice, cover, cook about 10 minutes or until just tender. Stir in flour, sugar and cinnamon; cool to room temperature.

Topping: Combine sugar, flour and pecans in bowl, rub in butter until mixture is coarse and crumbly.

■ **TO FREEZE:** Bake, cool and wrap flan in freezer wrap. Freeze for up to 2 months. Thaw in refrigerator overnight or at room temperature for 2 hours.

Note: This recipe is not suitable to microwave.

Glass platter is Mikasa Scala Gold.

COFFEE LIQUEUR MOUSSE

Mousse can be made up to 2 days ahead, covered and refrigerated.

1¼ cups brown sugar, lightly packed
½ cup water
2¼ cups milk
6 eggs, separated
¼ cup Tia Maria or Kahlua
1½ tablespoons instant coffee powder
2 tablespoons boiling water
2 tablespoons gelatine
⅓ cup cold water
2 cups thickened cream, whipped

Combine brown sugar and water in pan, stir constantly over heat without boiling until sugar is dissolved. Bring to boil, boil uncovered for about 10 minutes or until mixture is dark golden brown, then test by dropping a teaspoonful of toffee into a glass of cold water. If it is ready, toffee will set immediately it is tested. Remove from heat, add milk, stir until toffee is dissolved. It may be necessary to return to low heat to dissolve toffee completely. Stir in combined egg yolks, Tia Maria and combined coffee and boiling water. Sprinkle gelatine over cold water, dissolve over hot water, cool 5 minutes, stir into coffee mixture. Refrigerate until just beginning to set, stirring occasionally; fold in cream. Beat egg whites until soft peaks form, fold into coffee mixture. Place in serving dish, refrigerate overnight or for several hours until set. Decorate with extra whipped cream and chocolate curls (see page 7) if desired.

Note: This recipe is not suitable to freeze.

Right: Fruit Salad with Chantilly Cream. Far right: Chocolate, Walnut and Sour Cream Flan. Above right: Coffee Liqueur Mousse.

FRUIT SALAD WITH CHANTILLY CREAM

Choose a variety of good quality firm, ripe fruit in season. We used apples, passionfruit, pears, melon, strawberries, kiwi fruit, oranges and grapes. Prepare fruit and Cream, cover and refrigerate separately up to 12 hours before serving. Good quality prepared fruit salad is available from many shops; simply add a few more varieties of fresh colored fruit – such as strawberries, grapes, kiwi fruit, etc. – to give it the "just made" look.

1½kg fruit salad
¼ cup sugar
½ cup water
1 tablespoon Grand Marnier
   or brandy
CHANTILLY CREAM
2 × 300ml cartons thickened cream
⅓ cup sour cream
½ cup castor sugar
2 teaspoons vanilla
1 tablespoon Grand Marnier
   or brandy

Combine sugar and water in pan, stir over heat until sugar is dissolved; cool, add Grand Marnier. Toss fruit and Grand Marnier syrup together in large serving bowl, refrigerate, covered, until ready to serve with Chantilly Cream.
Chantilly Cream: Combine all ingredients in medium bowl, beat with electric mixer until soft peaks form, refrigerate, covered, until ready to serve.
Note: This recipe is not suitable to freeze.

CHOCOLATE, WALNUT AND SOUR CREAM FLAN

Make flan completely up to 2 days before required, if desired. Store, covered in refrigerator.

PASTRY
1 cup plain flour
1 tablespoon castor sugar
90g butter
1 egg yolk
1 tablespoon water, approximately
60g dark chocolate
FILLING
¾ cup sugar
¼ cup water
300ml carton sour cream
1 teaspoon vanilla
1 egg
1 egg yolk
125g unsalted butter, melted
1¾ cups (185g) chopped walnuts

Pastry: Sift flour into bowl, add sugar, rub in butter. Add egg yolk and enough water to mix ingredients together. Shape into ball, cover, refrigerate 30 minutes. Roll pastry large enough to line 23cm flan tin; trim edges. Bake blind by lining flan case with greaseproof paper and filling with dried peas, beans or rice, etc. Bake in moderately hot oven 7 minutes. Remove beans and paper carefully, return to oven, bake further 7 minutes; cool. Melt chocolate over hot water, brush inside of flan case with chocolate. Pour Filling into case, bake in moderate oven 30 minutes; cool. Decorate with melted chocolate (to make paper bags and to pipe chocolate, see page 11), cream and walnut halves, if desired.

Filling: Stir sugar and water in pan over heat without boiling until sugar is dissolved, bring to boil, boil rapidly without stirring for about 5 minutes or until light golden brown. Remove from heat, add cream. Return to heat, stir over low heat few minutes or until mixture is smooth; cool 15 minutes. Whisk in combined vanilla, egg and egg yolk, then butter and walnuts.

Note: This recipe is not suitable to freeze or microwave.

STRAWBERRY MOUSSE HAZELNUT TORTE

For best results make Torte completely up to a day before required. We recommend using home-ground roasted hazelnuts for this recipe.

HAZELNUT MERINGUE
3 egg whites
¾ cup castor sugar
1¾ cups (170g) roasted hazelnuts
¼ cup plain flour
STRAWBERRY MOUSSE
2 × 250g punnets strawberries
3 egg yolks
½ cup castor sugar
1 tablespoon gelatine
¼ cup water
2 × 300ml cartons thickened cream, whipped
pink food coloring

Hazelnut Meringue: Beat egg whites until soft peaks form, add sugar gradually, beat until sugar is dissolved. Blend or process hazelnuts until finely ground, combine with flour, fold into meringue. Spread half the mixture evenly over the base part only of a greased and floured 25cm springform pan. Bake in moderately slow oven 25 minutes, cool 5 minutes, remove from base with spatula, cool on wire rack. Repeat with remaining Hazelnut Meringue mixture.

Strawberry Mousse: Reserve some strawberries for decorating dessert. Puree remaining strawberries in processor or blender until smooth; pour into large bowl. Beat egg yolks and sugar in small bowl with electric mixer until pale and thick, fold into strawberry mixture. Sprinkle gelatine over water, dissolve over hot water, cool to room temperature, add to strawberry mixture; fold in half the whipped cream. Tint pale pink with food coloring, if desired.

To assemble:
STEP ONE
Place plastic food wrap over base of springform pan, top with one layer of Meringue, top side down.

STEP 2
Place springform side around base so plastic food wrap lines inside of pan completely. Pour Strawberry Mousse into pan.

STEP 3
Cover with remaining Hazelnut Meringue layer top side up, refrigerate overnight or several hours until set.

To Serve: Release springform side from pan, remove dessert, pull plastic food wrap away from side, invert dessert onto serving plate. Remove base and plastic, dust top with sifted icing sugar. Decorate with half the cream and reserved strawberries and extra chopped roasted hazelnuts, if desired.

Note: This recipe is not suitable to freeze or microwave.

Chinese food is quick and easy to cook, but it does take a little time to prepare; however, most of the chopping and slicing can be done well ahead of serving time. We suggest you serve the food in the order in which it appears in the menu.

CHINESE STYLE DINNER PARTY FOR SIX

PRAWN TOASTS

SPICY HAM AND CHICKEN PARCELS

STIR-FRY CHILLI BEEF

CRISPY SKIN CHICKEN WITH SPICED SALT

BROWN FRIED RICE WITH SHREDDED LETTUCE

SCHNAPPER WITH GINGER AND CARROTS

ALMOND JELLY IN ORANGE SYRUP

SWEET COCONUT TARTLETS

Prepare the desserts the day before required. Fry the savories just before you are ready to serve them. Serve only one course at a time. This way everything will be hot and have that wonderful, just-cooked flavor. It means more work for the cook but the compliments will be worth it. If you can organise two woks or large pans, it will be easier to cope.

Serve Sweet Coconut Tartlets with Chinese tea at the end of the meal. Teapot from Dansab.

PRAWN TOASTS

Prawn mixture can be made the day before required, covered and refrigerated, then spread on bread up to 2 hours before cooking.

500g green king prawns
⅓ cup slivered almonds, chopped
1 slice (30g) ham, finely chopped
4 green shallots, finely chopped
½ teaspoon sesame oil
2 teaspoons soy sauce
1 tablespoon plum sauce
8 slices thick white sandwich bread
oil for deep frying

STEP 1
Peel and devein prawns.

STEP 2
Chop prawns finely, combine with almonds, ham, shallots, sesame oil, soy and plum sauces. Remove crusts from bread, spread each slice with prawn mixture, cut into 3 finger-lengths.

STEP 3
Deep fry in hot oil until golden brown, turn during cooking. Drain on absorbent paper; serve immediately.

■ **TO FREEZE:** Prawn Toasts can be assembled, placed in single layer on tray, frozen, then wrapped in airtight bags and frozen for up to 4 weeks. Thaw for 30 minutes before cooking.
Note: This recipe is not suitable to microwave.
Makes 24.

SPICY HAM AND CHICKEN PARCELS

Parcels can be assembled and refrigerated, covered, for up to 2 hours before cooking.

2 chicken breast fillets
60g ham
4 green shallots
24 wonton wrappers
2 cloves garlic, crushed
¼ teaspoon five spice powder
¼ teaspoon black pepper
oil for deep frying

STEP 1
Cut chicken and ham into 4cm strips, cut shallots into 4cm lengths.

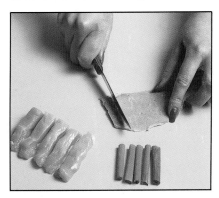

STEP 2
Place wonton wrappers on bench, spread each with a little combined garlic, five spice powder and pepper.

STEP 3
Place a piece of chicken, ham and shallot across corner of each wrapper, roll up, tucking in ends. Brush edge with a little water.

STEP 4
Deep fry in hot oil until cooked through and golden brown, drain on absorbent paper; serve immediately.

■ **TO FREEZE:** Place uncooked parcels on tray in single layer, freeze, place in airtight bag, freeze for up to 4 weeks. Thaw at least 30 minutes before cooking.
Note: This recipe is not suitable to microwave.
Makes 24.

Back: Prawn Toasts.
Front: Spicy Ham and Chicken Parcels.
Plate at back is Galleria Spectra
Black from Mikasa; plate and chopsticks in front are from Dansab; background fabric is Chopsticks Onyx by Wilson.

STIR-FRY CHILLI BEEF

Sauce can be made a day ahead of time and ingredients prepared. Partly freeze beef for easy slicing.

500g beef eye fillet in one piece
8 (250g) baby new potatoes
2 medium carrots
½ x 300ml can bamboo shoots
125g baby mushrooms
4 green shallots
2 tablespoons oil
SAUCE
¼ cup light soy sauce
1 teaspoon finely grated orange rind
⅓ cup orange juice
1 clove garlic, crushed
1 teaspoon cornflour
1 small red chilli, finely chopped

STEP 1

Remove fat and sinew from beef, cut beef into thin slices across the grain, then cut slices in half again.

STEP 2

Finely slice unpeeled potatoes, slice carrots diagonally; slice bamboo shoots thinly. Quarter mushrooms, slice shallots diagonally.

STEP 3

Heat oil in wok or pan, add beef, stir-fry over high heat until meat is lightly browned, remove from pan. Add potatoes, stir-fry few minutes, add carrots, stir-fry few minutes; add mushrooms and bamboo shoots, then Sauce and beef. Stir-fry until mixture boils and thickens and vegetables are just tender. Sprinkle with shallots just before serving. Serve immediately.

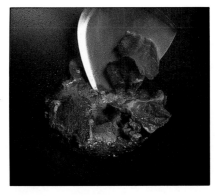

Sauce: Combine all ingredients.
Note: This recipe is not suitable to freeze or microwave.

CRISPY SKIN CHICKEN WITH SPICED SALT

Size 13 chicken
1 tablespoon golden syrup
2 teaspoons dark soy sauce
oil for deep frying
SPICED SALT
1 tablespoon coarse kitchen salt
¼ teaspoon five spice powder

STEP 1

Remove any fat from inside of chicken. Lower chicken into pan of boiling salted water, return to boil, turn heat off. Cover pan, stand 30 minutes; remove chicken from water, pat chicken dry with absorbent paper.

STEP 2

Combine golden syrup with soy sauce, brush chicken evenly with syrup mixture, stand 10 minutes. Brush again with remaining syrup mixture. Refrigerate chicken overnight uncovered on wire rack over tray.

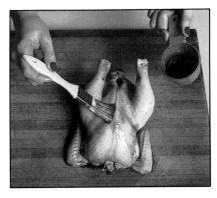

STEP 3

Next day, cut chicken in half lengthwise, then place on wire ladle with skin side up. Heat oil (oil should be about 8cm deep) in wok, lower chicken gently into oil, leaving ladle under chicken. Spoon hot oil constantly over exposed part of chicken until it is golden brown; this takes about 10 minutes. Repeat with remaining half of chicken. Cool slightly, cut chicken into serving-sized pieces. Serve with Spiced Salt.

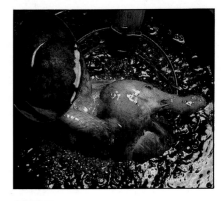

STEP 4

Spiced Salt: Place salt and five spice powder into small pan, stir over low heat for 2 minutes.

Note: This recipe is not suitable to freeze or microwave.

Back: Crispy Skin Chicken with Spiced Salt.
Front: Stir-Fry Chilli Beef.
Plate at back is Hakusan Dots — Black from Dansab; plate in front is Galleria Spectra Black from Mikasa.

BROWN FRIED RICE WITH SHREDDED LETTUCE

Rice can be prepared up to 4 days before serving. The rest of the recipe can be completed up to 2 hours before serving. Stir-fry in wok until hot.

⅔ cup brown rice
3 eggs
½ teaspoon sesame oil
2 teaspoons oil
1 tablespoon oil, extra
2 teaspoons grated fresh ginger
250g Chinese barbecued pork, finely chopped
8 green shallots, chopped
500g cooked prawns, shelled
1 small lettuce, shredded
1 tablespoon light soy sauce

STEP 1

Add rice gradually to large pan of boiling water, boil rapidly uncovered for 25 minutes or until just tender. Drain, rinse under cold water, drain well. Place rice on 2 oven trays, bake in moderate oven 20 minutes; stir every 5 minutes; cool, refrigerate until ready to cook. Beat eggs with sesame oil. Heat 1 teaspoon of the oil in wok or pan, pour in enough egg mixture to make 1 small omelette, turn, cook other side, remove from pan, repeat with remaining oil and egg mixture. Roll up omelettes, slice into thin strips.

STEP 2

Heat extra oil in wok, add rice and ginger, stir-fry few minutes.

STEP 3

Add pork, shallots, prawns, lettuce and omelette strips, stir-fry few minutes, add soy sauce, serve immediately.

Note: This recipe is not suitable to freeze or microwave.

SCHNAPPER WITH GINGER AND CARROTS

Cook this recipe as close to serving time as possible. Fish cannot be reheated successfully.

2 whole schnapper (about 500g each)
cornflour
2 teaspoons oil
4 carrots
1 onion
4cm piece green ginger, peeled
½ teaspoon sesame oil
2 tablespoons light soy sauce
2 teaspoons cornflour, extra
1 tablespoon dry sherry
1½ cups water
6 green shallots

STEP 1

Trim fins and tail of fish. Cut a few slashes in each side of fish, rub both sides of fish with cornflour.

Back: Brown Fried Rice with Shredded Lettuce.
Front: Schnapper with Ginger and Carrots. Platter and bowl are Ribbon of Gold by Mikasa.

STEP 2

Cut carrots, onion and ginger into thin strips. Heat oil in wok, add carrots and onion, stir-fry until just tender, add ginger, cook 1 minute.

STEP 3

Push vegetables to one side, add fish, pour half the combined sesame oil and soy sauce over fish, cook 5 minutes. When brown, turn fish over, add remaining sesame and soy mixture.

STEP 4

Pour blended extra cornflour, sherry and water over fish, stir gently 1 minute or until mixture boils. Cover, cook gently 5 minutes or until fish is tender. Add shallots in last few minutes of cooking time.

Note: This recipe is not suitable to freeze or microwave.

ALMOND JELLY IN ORANGE SYRUP

Make jelly up to 2 days ahead of serving time, if desired. Serve jelly with fruit of your choice. We used fresh sliced kiwi fruit, orange segments (see page 117) and canned lychees.

2 tablespoons gelatine
1¼ cups cold water
1¼ cups boiling water
2⅓ cups milk
½ cup sugar
2 teaspoons almond essence
ORANGE SYRUP
1 cup orange juice
½ cup water
1 cup castor sugar

STEP 1

Place cold water in bowl, add gelatine, stand few minutes; stir in boiling water, stir until gelatine is dissolved.

STEP 2

Add milk, sugar and almond essence, stir until sugar is dissolved. Pour into lamington tin (base measures 16cm x 26cm), refrigerate several hours or overnight until jelly is set.

Back: Sweet Coconut Tartlets.
Front: Almond Jelly in Orange Syrup.

STEP 3

Cut jelly into diamond shapes with hot wet knife; serve with fruit and Orange Syrup.

Orange Syrup: Combine orange juice, water and sugar in pan, stir over heat until sugar is dissolved, without boiling. Bring to the boil, boil few minutes without stirring, cool, refrigerate before serving over Almond Jelly.
Note: This recipe is not suitable to freeze.

SWEET COCONUT TARTLETS

Store tartlets in airtight container for up to 4 days, if desired.

PASTRY
1 cup plain flour
½ cup self-raising flour
2 tablespoons castor sugar
125g cold butter, chopped
1 egg
1 tablespoon water
apricot jam
red glace cherries
FILLING
1 cup water
1 cup sugar
3½ cups coconut
3 eggs, lightly beaten
60g butter, melted
3 tablespoons milk
1 teaspoon vanilla
1 teaspoon baking powder

STEP 1

Pastry: Combine flours, sugar and butter in processor, process until combined. Add egg and water, process until mixture forms a ball, cover, refrigerate 30 minutes. Roll pastry out thinly between 2 sheets of plastic food wrap. Cut out pieces of pastry to line 18 deep tartlet tins (base measures 5cm). Place ½ teaspoon jam in each pastry case.

STEP 2

Filling: Combine water and sugar in pan, stir over heat until sugar is dissolved. Bring to boil, boil 3 minutes without stirring; cool 5 minutes. Place coconut in bowl, add sugar syrup, eggs, butter, milk, vanilla and baking powder, mix well.

STEP 3

Spoon coconut mixture evenly into pastry cases.

STEP 4

Top each tartlet with a piece of glace cherry. Bake in moderate oven 30 minutes. Cool 5 minutes before removing from tins to wire rack to cool.

■ **TO FREEZE:** Freeze cooked tartlets covered for up to 2 weeks. Thaw at room temperature.
Note: This recipe is not suitable to microwave.
Makes 18.

Pleasing 10 children is easy with these recipes. Most of the recipes can be made well ahead of party time to save last-minute worries. The Frog in the Pond cake we've made can be for a boy or a girl.

CHILDREN'S PARTY FOR 10

CRISPY CHICKEN WINGS

COLD PINEAPPLE BEEF PATTIES

SAUCY CORN DOGS ON A STICK

SLOPPY JOES

CRUNCHY TUNA POCKETS

MONKEY TAILS

COCONUT CHERRY SLICE

FAIRY CAKES

CORNFLAKE COCONUT CUPS

NUTTY POPCORN TOFFEES

FROG IN THE POND CAKE

CRISPY CHICKEN WINGS

This recipe can be prepared to the stage of cooking up to 4 hours ahead; cover, refrigerate, cook just before serving for crispiest results.

15 chicken wings
3 cups stale breadcrumbs
½ cup grated parmesan cheese
4 green shallots, finely chopped
1 teaspoon paprika
2 eggs, lightly beaten
⅓ cup milk
125g butter, melted

Combine breadcrumbs with cheese, shallots and paprika. Dip chicken wings in combined egg and milk, coat with breadcrumb mixture. Place in ovenproof dish in single layer, drizzle with butter, bake in moderately hot oven 30 minutes or until chicken is tender and golden brown. Do not turn chicken during cooking.
Makes 15.
Note: This recipe is not suitable to freeze or microwave.

From left: Saucy Corn Dogs on a Stick; Sloppy Joes; Cold Pineapple Beef Patties; Crispy Chicken Wings.
China is Mobile by Thomas from Swift Consumer Products; tumblers are Cole and Mason from Vasa Agencies.

COLD PINEAPPLE BEEF PATTIES

Prepare and cook up to 2 days before required. Keep refrigerated for up to a week. Serve cold with dipping Sauce.

500g topside mince
250g sausage mince
440g can crushed pineapple
1 cup stale breadcrumbs
1 small green pepper, finely chopped
½ cup tomato sauce
1 teaspoon chilli sauce
plain flour
oil for shallow frying
SAUCE
½ cup mayonnaise
2 tablespoons tomato sauce

Drain pineapple, reserve ¼ cup syrup for Sauce. Add pineapple to mince, breadcrumbs, pepper and sauces; mix well. Shape into 15 patties, coat lightly with flour, fry in hot oil until browned both sides and cooked through; cool before serving.
Sauce: Combine mayonnaise with tomato sauce and reserved syrup.
Makes 15.
■ **TO FREEZE:** Freeze in airtight container when cold for up to 2 months.
Note: This recipe is not suitable to microwave.

SAUCY CORN DOGS ON A STICK

Ask your butcher for thick wooden skewers for this recipe. Skewer frankfurts several hours before cooking. Prepare batter up to an hour before required.

20 cocktail frankfurts
1 cup polenta (cornmeal)
½ cup self-raising flour, sifted
2 tablespoons sugar
½ cup grated tasty cheese
½ cup milk
2 eggs, lightly beaten
60g butter, melted
oil for deep frying
SAUCE
½ cup tomato sauce
2 tablespoons grainy mustard
2 tablespoons finely chopped gherkins

Cut off points from wooden skewers. Insert skewer into each frankfurt. Combine polenta, flour, sugar and cheese in bowl, make well in centre. Add combined milk, eggs and butter; stir until well combined. Dip frankfurts into batter, deep fry in hot oil 2 minutes or until batter is brown. Drain on absorbent paper, serve with Sauce.
Sauce: Combine tomato sauce, mustard and gherkins.
Note: This recipe is not suitable to freeze or microwave.

SLOPPY JOES

Sloppy Joes are named for the mess they create on your windcheater. They are fun to eat and taste great too! Use wholemeal bread rolls in place of hamburger buns, if desired.

500g minced steak
1 tablespoon oil
1 onion, chopped
2 sticks celery, chopped
2 × 440g cans baked beans in tomato sauce
½ cup tomato sauce
¼ cup barbecue sauce
6 hamburger buns, split

Heat oil in pan, add onion and celery, cook stirring until onion is soft. Add mince, cook stirring until well browned; pour off excess oil. Add baked beans, tomato sauce and barbecue sauce, bring to boil, reduce heat, simmer uncovered 15 minutes or until mince is cooked. Pour over toasted hamburger bun halves.
■ **TO MICROWAVE:** Cook oil, onion and celery in large bowl on HIGH 3 minutes. Add mince, cook on HIGH 6 minutes, breaking up mince with a fork. Add remaining ingredients, cook on HIGH 5 minutes or until heated through. Serve as above.
■ **TO FREEZE:** Cook as above, cool, store in airtight container, freeze for up to 2 months. To use, thaw on top of the stove over low heat or in microwave on defrost low cycle.

CRUNCHY TUNA POCKETS

Filling can be made the day before, refrigerated and reheated when required.

30g butter
1 large onion, finely chopped
1½ tablespoons plain flour
½ teaspoon curry powder
1 cup milk
1 stick celery, chopped
1 tomato, chopped
425g can chunk style tuna, drained
5 pocket breads
1 cup finely shredded lettuce

Melt butter in pan, add onion, saute until soft. Stir in flour and curry powder, cook 1 minute, add milk, stir over heat until mixture boils and thickens. Stir in celery, tuna and tomato. Place bread pockets onto oven tray, bake in moderate oven 10 minutes or until hot. Cut bread in half crosswise to give 2 pockets. Spoon lettuce into pockets, top with hot tuna mixture; serve with potato crisps, if desired.

Makes 10.

■ **TO MICROWAVE:** Combine butter and onion in shallow dish, cook on HIGH 4 minutes or until onion is soft. Add flour and curry powder, cook on HIGH 1 minute. Add milk, cook on HIGH 3 minutes or until mixture boils and thickens, stirring occasionally. Proceed as above.

Note: This recipe is not suitable to freeze.

MONKEY TAILS

These will keep covered and refrigerated for up to a week. Use flat wooden sticks.

10 firm ripe bananas
200g dark chocolate, chopped
2 tablespoons oil
1 cup finely chopped mixed nuts

Toast nuts on oven tray in moderate oven for about 5 minutes, cool. Peel bananas, insert stick into each banana. Melt chocolate over hot water; stir in oil. Place nuts on a sheet of greaseproof paper. Dip bananas in chocolate mixture, 1 at a time, using a spoon to coat them evenly; sprinkle thickly with nuts, place on oven tray, refrigerate until set.

Makes 10.

■ **TO FREEZE:** Freeze Monkey Tails covered for up to 4 weeks.

Above: Crunchy Tuna Pockets.
Below: Monkey Tails.
Opposite Page: left, Fairy Cakes; right, Coconut Cherry Slice.

COCONUT CHERRY SLICE

This slice will keep in an airtight container in refrigerator for up to a week.

1 cup self-raising flour
⅓ cup castor sugar
¼ cup coconut
125g butter, melted
¼ cup plum jam
TOPPING
125g glace cherries
1 cup coconut
¼ cup sugar
1 tablespoon cornflour
1 egg, lightly beaten

Sift flour into bowl, add sugar and coconut, mix in butter. Press mixture evenly into lamington tin (base measures 16cm × 26cm), bake in moderate oven 15 minutes or until light golden brown, cool in tin. Brush base with plum jam, sprinkle with Topping. Bake in moderate oven 20 minutes, cool in tin before cutting.

Topping: Chop cherries finely in processor. Combine in bowl with coconut, sugar and cornflour, mix in egg.

Note: This recipe is not suitable to freeze or microwave.

FAIRY CAKES

To prevent cakes from "peaking", place tray of cakes on shelf position in the lower half of the oven, usually on the second shelf from the bottom. Place an oven tray on 1 or 2 shelf positions above the cakes in the upper half of the oven, usually the fourth shelf position from the bottom of the oven. Cakes can be made completely a day before required.

125g butter
1 teaspoon vanilla
¾ cup castor sugar
3 eggs
1½ cups self-raising flour
½ cup custard powder
¼ cup milk
CREAM CHEESE TOPPING
250g packet cream cheese, softened
3 cups icing sugar, sifted
2 teaspoons vanilla
1 tablespoon grated lemon rind
½ cup hundreds and thousands

Beat butter, vanilla and sugar in small bowl with electric mixer until light and creamy. Beat in eggs 1 at a time; mixture might curdle at this stage but will reconstitute later. Add combined sifted flour and custard powder and milk; beat until just combined and smooth. Drop level tablespoons of mixture into greased patty pans with rounded bases. Bake in moderate oven for 15 minutes or until light golden brown. Turn onto wire rack to cool. Spread rounded base of each cake with Cream Cheese Topping, roll in hundreds and thousands.

Cream Cheese Topping: Place cream cheese in processor, process until smooth; while motor is operating, add icing sugar, vanilla and lemon rind, process until smooth.

Makes about 45.

■ **TO FREEZE:** Undecorated cakes can be wrapped in an airtight bag and frozen for up to 8 weeks. Decorate while frozen, if desired.

Note: This recipe is not suitable to microwave.

CORNFLAKE COCONUT CUPS

Prepare up to a day ahead of the party. Keep covered in refrigerator.

4 cups cornflakes
1 cup coconut
⅔ cup brown sugar
⅓ cup honey
¼ cup lemon juice
185g butter
extra coconut

Combine cornflakes and coconut in bowl. Combine brown sugar, honey, lemon juice and butter in pan, stir over heat without boiling until sugar is dissolved. Increase heat, boil 5 minutes without stirring or until mixture thickens (enough to coat the back of a spoon). Pour sugar mixture into cornflake mixture, mix well.

Drop tablespoons of mixture into paper patty cases in patty pans, sprinkle with extra coconut, refrigerate until set.

Makes 24.

Note: This recipe is not suitable to freeze or microwave.

NUTTY POPCORN TOFFEES

2 tablespoons oil
½ cup popping corn
¾ cup unsalted roasted peanuts
3 cups sugar
1 cup water

Heat oil in large pan, add corn, cook covered over high heat until corn pops, about 3 minutes. Divide corn and peanuts between lightly greased patty pans. Combine sugar and water in pan, stir over low heat until sugar dissolves, bring to boil, boil rapidly without stirring for about 10 minutes or until golden brown. Pour toffee over popcorn mixture. Leave until set, remove from patty pans, store in an airtight container for up to 3 days.

Makes 24.

Note: This recipe is not suitable to freeze or microwave.

Above: Cornflake Coconut Cups.
Below: Nutty Popcorn Toffees.

FROG IN THE POND

20cm round cake
Rocky Road
125g dark chocolate, melted
12 × 100g packets lime jelly
licorice, marshmallows, Smarties, mint leaves
chocolate fish and turtles
VIENNA CREAM
125g butter, softened
1½ cups icing sugar, sifted
2 tablespoons milk
green food coloring

Make or buy a sponge or butter cake for the frog. Make a pattern for the frog by folding a piece of greaseproof paper in half and tracing the outline shown on this page. Cut out pattern, unfold to use. Freeze cake for about 1 hour to make cutting out easier. Make the pond up to 2 days before the party, keep refrigerated if weather is hot. The jelly will remain set at room temperature during the cooler months. Choose a large tray or board that will accommodate the pond; ours measured about 30cm × 40cm. Remember to check that the tray will fit into the refrigerator, if necessary. Cut Rocky Road into strips to make a border for the pond, join Rocky Road pieces with chocolate, patch any holes in the "wall" with more chocolate, allow to set. Make jellies, using half the amount of water specified on the packet, that is, 12 cups or 3 litres of water. Refrigerate until jelly is set slightly; it must still be pourable. Pour a thin layer of jelly into pond, allow to set. Leave remaining jelly out of refrigerator to prevent further setting. Place chocolate fish on set jelly, top with remaining jelly; allow to set.

To make the frog
STEP 1
Using pattern, cut out shape of frog, as shown.

STEP 2
Using leftover cake, cut out one cheek of frog.

STEP 3
Using remaining cake, cut out other cheek of frog.

STEP 4
Place strip of licorice in position to represent mouth, secure cheeks to head of frog with toothpicks. Using knife, contour shape of head, as shown.

Join cheeks to head with a little Vienna Cream, spread top of frog's head and under throat with dark green Vienna Cream. Spread throat of frog with light green Vienna Cream. Use licorice for mouth. Place frog in position on pond. Make eyes with marshmallows and licorice, decorate with Smarties.

Decorate pond with sweets, as shown.

Vienna Cream: Beat butter in small bowl with electric mixer until light and creamy. Beat in half the icing sugar, then remaining icing sugar and milk, color two-thirds of the Cream dark green and remaining Cream light green.

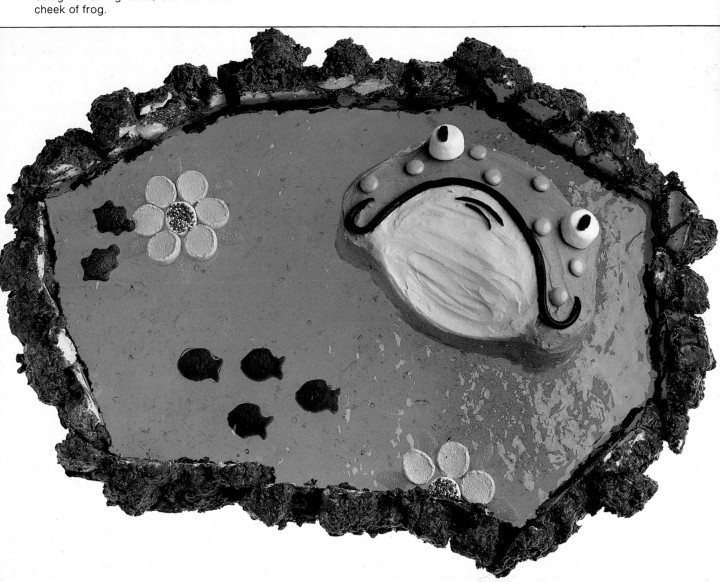

There are many occasions when it is perfect to serve an elegant lunch; this menu is especially impressive. It will take a little time to prepare the day before, but last minute details are minimal.

CHAMPAGNE LUNCH FOR 10

ASPARAGUS CREAM CHEESE PATE

BRIOCHE WITH SEAFOOD AND SPINACH FILLING

SEASONED PHEASANT WITH PRUNES IN PORT

WILD RICE AND BROWN RICE SALAD

LEAFY GREEN SALAD WITH FRESH HERB LEMON DRESSING

CHOCOLATE STRAWBERRIES IN TOFFEE BASKET WITH CREME FRAICHE

ASPARAGUS CREAM CHEESE PATE

Pate is best made 2 to 3 days before serving. Keep covered in refrigerator.

340g can green asparagus spears, drained
250g packet cream cheese, softened
2 teaspoons grated lemon rind
2 tablespoons sour cream
30g butter, softened
2 teaspoons french mustard

Puree asparagus in processor until smooth, remove from bowl. Process cream cheese with lemon rind, sour cream, butter and mustard until smooth. While motor is operating add asparagus gradually through chute, process until smooth; spread into serving dish, cover, refrigerate several hours or overnight.
Note: This recipe is not suitable to freeze.

SEASONED PHEASANT WITH PRUNES IN PORT

Cook pheasant up to 3 days before serving. Keep covered in refrigerator. You will need to buy a piece of cheesecloth (available from some specialty kitchenware shops and department stores), measuring about 38cm × 88cm.

No. 11 pheasant
375g pork and veal mince
125g ham, minced
2 tablespoons pinenuts
8 pitted prunes
⅓ cup port
1 onion, chopped
1 clove garlic, crushed
30g butter
½ cup chopped parsley
1 egg, lightly beaten
3 bacon rashers
2½ litres (10 cups) water
1 carrot, chopped
1 onion, chopped
few black peppercorns

Toast pinenuts on oven tray in moderate oven for about 5 minutes. Soak prunes in port several hours; drain. Saute onion and garlic in butter for 2 minutes. Combine onion mixture, mince, ham, parsley and egg in bowl, stir in pinenuts.

STEP 1

Cut off wing tips of pheasant at second joint. Cut off neck; reserve bones for stock. Cut through skin of pheasant down centre breast. Separate flesh from breastbone on one side with tip of knife. Then, following shape of bones of pheasant, gradually ease flesh away from bones. Repeat process with other side of pheasant. Holding ribcage away from pheasant, gently cut away. Hold up thigh with one hand, cut around top of bone to remove flesh, scrape down the bone to next joint, cut around flesh again, scrape down to end. Pull bone out and cut

away. Repeat this process with other leg bone and with both wings. Place bones in large pan, add water, carrot, onion and peppercorns. Bring to boil, reduce heat, simmer covered 1 hour; strain, discard bones and vegetables.

STEP 2

Turn flesh of legs and wings inside pheasant. Place bacon over pheasant and trim to cover flesh, as shown. Press half the meat mixture down centre of pheasant, place prunes down centre, as shown, then cover with remaining meat mixture. Place remaining trimmed bacon over meat, fold one side of pheasant over bacon, then other side. Sew flesh together with needle and thread.

STEP 3

Fold cheesecloth in half crosswise, place pheasant at one end and roll up. Tie with string at 5cm intervals to keep shape while cooking.

STEP 4

Place stock in pan, bring to boil, add pheasant, reduce heat, simmer covered 1¼ hours. Cool pheasant in stock. Refrigerate wrapped in foil overnight. Remove string, cloth and thread, cut into thin slices to serve.

■ **TO FREEZE:** Freeze uncooked Seasoned Pheasant for up to 2 weeks. Thaw in refrigerator 24 hours before baking.
Note: This recipe is not suitable to microwave.

BRIOCHE WITH SEAFOOD AND SPINACH FILLING

Individual brioche can be prepared the day before to the point of placing the dough into the moulds; cover, refrigerate until next day, allow to come to room temperature, proceed as below. This recipe will need 12 individual ½-cup moulds. If only 6 moulds are available, cook 6 brioche; remaining dough can be left covered in the refrigerator until ready to cook remaining brioche. One large brioche can be made from this recipe. You will required a 6½-cup mould. Bake in moderately hot oven for 10 minutes, reduce to moderate, bake further 45 minutes or until brioche sounds hollow when tapped on the top. Large brioche often brown too much; cover after about 30 minutes to help prevent this happening. Brioche, large or small, can be made up to 12 hours before filling, reheating and serving.

BRIOCHE
15g compressed yeast
2 tablespoons sugar
½ cup warm water
4 cups plain flour
1 teaspoon salt
4 eggs, lightly beaten
185g butter, softened
1 egg yolk, extra
¼ cup cream

SEAFOOD FILLING
500g green king prawns, shelled
250g white fish fillets
125g scallops
12 oysters
3 cups water
1 cup dry white wine
1 bay leaf
1 small onion, finely chopped
30g butter
125g baby mushrooms, sliced
¼ cup plain flour
300ml carton cream
250g packet frozen chopped spinach, thawed
1 cup grated tasty cheese

Brioche
STEP 1

Cream yeast with 1 teaspoon of the sugar, add warm water, let stand in a warm place about 10 minutes or until frothy. Sift flour, salt and remaining sugar into large basin; stir in combined eggs and yeast mixture. Turn onto lightly floured surface, knead mixture for about 3 minutes; mixture will be dry. Work in butter gradually, knead until dough is smooth and elastic, about 10 minutes.

STEP 2

Place in lightly greased bowl, cover with plastic food wrap, stand in warm place for 1 hour or until dough is doubled in bulk. Knock dough back, knead until smooth. Divide dough into 12 portions. Grease fluted moulds (½-cup capacity). Remove ¼ of the dough from each portion. Mould the larger portions into rounds, place in moulds.

STEP 3

Shape smaller portions of dough into rounds. Brush dough in moulds with combined extra egg yolk and cream. Place small rounds of dough on top of dough in moulds. Using a wooden skewer, push dough from the top of the small round through to the base of the mould. This ensures that the small round will stay in position. Brush with remaining egg yolk and cream, stand in warm place for about 15 minutes or until doubled in size. Bake in moderately hot oven 10 minutes, reduce heat to moderate, bake further 10 minutes or until brioche sounds hollow when tapped on the top. Remove from oven, turn out of moulds.

STEP 4

Cut tops from each brioche, scoop out inside, spoon in Filling, replace tops, stand on oven tray, cover with foil, heat in moderate oven 10 to 15 minutes.

Seafood Filling: Devein prawns, remove skin and bones from fish, clean scallops, remove oysters from shell. Combine water, wine and bay leaf in large pan, cover, simmer 10 minutes. Add seafood, simmer few minutes or until just done, remove seafood. Strain stock, reserve ½ cup for sauce. Combine onion and butter in pan, cook stirring until onions are soft. Add mushrooms, cook stirring until just tender, add flour, cook stirring few minutes. Stir in reserved stock, stir over heat until sauce boils and thickens; stir in cream, bring back to the boil. Remove from heat, add well drained spinach and cheese, stir until cheese is melted. Gently stir in seafood.

■ **TO FREEZE:** Baked unfilled brioche can be frozen for up to 2 months. Allow to come to room temperature, proceed as above. Seafood Filling is not suitable to freeze.

Note: This recipe is not suitable to microwave.

WILD RICE AND BROWN RICE SALAD

Salad can be prepared a day before required, keep covered and refrigerated. Add Dressing just before serving.

200g packet wild rice
1½ cups brown rice
6 green shallots, chopped
½ cucumber
1 red pepper, chopped
½ cup chopped parsley
DRESSING
1 tablespoon sugar
3 teaspoons curry powder
¾ cup oil
1½ tablespoons white vinegar

Add wild and brown rice gradually to large pan of boiling water, boil rapidly uncovered for 30 minutes; drain, rinse under cold water, drain well. Combine rice and shallots in bowl. Cut cucumber in half, scoop out seeds with teaspoon, slice cucumber thinly and add to rice with pepper and parsley. Before serving, stir Dressing through rice.
Dressing: Combine all ingredients.
Note: This recipe is not suitable to freeze or microwave.

LEAFY GREEN SALAD WITH FRESH HERB LEMON DRESSING

We used a combination of chives, parsley and basil for the Dressing. Use whatever fresh herbs are available. Greens and Dressing can be prepared and refrigerated separately the night before the lunch, if desired.

1 cos lettuce
1 mignonette lettuce
1 bunch curly endive
1 bunch English spinach
FRESH HERB LEMON DRESSING
⅓ cup finely chopped fresh herbs
⅓ cup lemon juice
⅔ cup olive oil
1 clove garlic, crushed
2 teaspoons french mustard

Wash and dry greens thoroughly; tear leaves into pieces, place into salad bowl, add Fresh Herb Lemon Dressing just before serving; toss well.
Fresh Herb Lemon Dressing: Combine all ingredients in a screwtop jar, shake well before serving.

Above: Wild Rice and Brown Rice Salad.
Below: Brioche with Seafood and Spinach Filling and Leafy Green Salad with Fresh Herb Lemon Dressing.
China is Fitz and Floyd Renaissance from Austfloyd.

CHOCOLATE STRAWBERRIES IN TOFFEE BASKET WITH CREME FRAICHE

Basket can be made up to 12 hours ahead of serving time. Fruit can be dipped up to a day ahead and refrigerated. Creme fraiche can be made up to 10 days ahead. Fill Basket with fruit just before serving. The pudding basin we used was of 8-cup capacity.

2 cups sugar
⅔ cup water
2 tablespoons brown vinegar
CHOCOLATE STRAWBERRIES
250g dark chocolate, chopped
4 × 250g punnets strawberries
CREME FRAICHE
300ml carton thickened cream
300ml carton sour cream

STEP 1

Combine sugar, water and vinegar in large, heavy based pan, stir over heat without boiling until sugar is dissolved. Bring to boil, boil uncovered without stirring for about 15 minutes or until toffee is golden brown and a teaspoon of toffee will crack when dropped into a cup of cold water. Stand toffee for about 10 minutes or until it has thickened slightly. Stand pan in a baking dish of hot water over low heat. Lightly oil a large pudding basin. Hold basin over pan; using a wooden spoon, drizzle toffee in thin stream, backward and forward, over sides and base of basin. Make rim of Basket a little thicker for added strength.

STEP 2

When toffee is set, carefully slide Basket from basin.

Chocolate Strawberries: Melt chocolate in bowl over hot water. Holding onto strawberry stems, dip half of strawberry into chocolate, hold over chocolate to allow excess to run off. Place onto foil-covered tray, refrigerate until set.

Creme Fraiche: Combine cream and sour cream, cover, leave unrefrigerated until thick; this will take 2 or 3 days, depending on weather. Refrigerate until required; will keep up to 1 week in refrigerator.

To serve, place strawberries and pieces of Toffee Basket on dessert plates, serve Creme Fraiche in a separate bowl for dipping.

Note: This recipe is not suitable to freeze or microwave.

An afternoon tea party is a delightful way to entertain a group of friends. Bring out your prettiest china and linen, then surprise your guests with your baking ability. We've chosen five sweet recipes, most of which can be made in advance.

AFTERNOON TEA PARTY FOR 10

There are enough goodies here to serve at least ten people; offer a variety of teas to please all tastes. Make some tiny sandwiches and Cheese-Topped Scones for those who like savory foods.

CHOCOLATE VANILLA CUSTARD SLICE

Complete Slice up to 48 hours before required, cover, refrigerate.

375g packet frozen puff pastry, thawed
CUSTARD
¾ cup sugar
⅔ cup cornflour
⅓ cup custard powder
4 cups milk
60g butter
2 egg yolks
2 teaspoons vanilla
60g dark chocolate, finely chopped
CHOCOLATE ICING
1 cup icing sugar
2 tablespoons cocoa
1 teaspoon soft butter
1 tablespoon water, approximately
¼ cup chopped walnuts

Halve pastry, roll out to 20cm × 30cm rectangle, trim edges. Place pastry on ungreased oven tray, bake in very hot oven 5 minutes or until brown. Trim pastry to cover base of lamington tin (base measures 16cm × 26cm). Roll remaining pastry to 23cm × 33cm rectangle, bake as above, cut to same size as top of tin. Line tin with foil. Place smaller piece of pastry into tin, puffy side up, flatten with hand. Drop spoonfuls of both flavors of hot Custard over pastry, top with flattened remaining pastry, puffy side down. Top with Icing, then walnuts. Cool, refrigerate overnight.

Custard: Combine sugar, cornflour and custard powder in pan, stir in milk. Stir constantly over heat until mixture boils and thickens, reduce heat, simmer stirring for 2 minutes. Remove from heat, stir in butter, egg yolks and vanilla. Divide Custard into 2 bowls, stir chocolate into 1 bowl of Custard.

Chocolate Icing: Sift icing sugar and cocoa into bowl, stir in butter and enough water to make a stiff paste. Stir over hot water until spreadable.

Note: This recipe is not suitable to freeze or microwave.

CHEESE-TOPPED SCONES

1½ cups self-raising flour
1 teaspoon icing sugar
30g butter
⅓ cup grated tasty cheese
¼ cup milk
½ cup water, approximately
30g butter, melted, extra
⅔ cup grated tasty cheese, extra

Sift flour and icing sugar into bowl, rub in butter and cheese. Make well in centre of dry ingredients, add milk, then stir in enough water to mix to a soft sticky dough. Turn dough onto lightly floured surface, knead lightly until smooth. Press dough out with hand to 1.5cm thickness, cut into rounds with sharp 5cm cutter. Place scones into well greased 20cm sandwich tin. Brush with extra butter; sprinkle evenly with extra cheese. Bake in hot oven 20 minutes or until golden brown. Serve hot with butter.

Makes about 12.

■ **TO FREEZE:** Wrap cold scones in single layer in foil, freeze for up to 2 months, heat, frozen, wrapped in foil, in moderate oven for about 20 minutes.

Note: This recipe is not suitable to microwave.

FUDGY PEANUT BUTTER CAKE

Cake can be made a day before required; store in airtight container.

125g butter
⅓ cup smooth peanut butter
⅓ cup brown sugar
⅓ cup castor sugar
1 egg
1½ cups self-raising flour
⅔ cup sour cream
CHOCOLATE FILLING
100g dark chocolate, chopped
**¼ cup canned sweetened
    condensed milk**
**½ cup chopped roasted
    unsalted peanuts**

Cream butter, peanut butter, sugars and egg in small bowl with electric mixer until light and creamy. Stir in sifted flour alternately with sour cream. Spread half the cake mixture into greased and floured 20cm baba or ring tin, spread evenly with Chocolate Filling, then top with remaining cake mixture. Bake in moderate oven 1 hour. Cool in tin 10 minutes before turning onto wire rack to cool. If desired, dust with sifted icing sugar when cold.
Chocolate Filling: Melt chocolate over hot water, stir in condensed milk and peanuts; use while warm.
■ **TO FREEZE:** Seal cake and freeze for up to 2 months.
Note: This recipe is not suitable to microwave.

ALMOND HEART BISCUITS

These biscuits will keep for about 2 weeks stored in an airtight container.

60g butter
2 tablespoons icing sugar, sifted
½ cup plain flour, sifted
¼ cup ground almonds
**1 tablespoon ground rice or rice
    flour**
½ cup flaked almonds
ICING
½ egg white
½ cup icing sugar, sifted
½ teaspoon plain flour
pink food coloring

Toast flaked almonds on oven tray in moderately slow oven for 10 minutes; cool. Cream butter and icing sugar in small bowl with electric mixer until light and fluffy. Stir in flour, ground almonds and ground rice. Knead lightly on floured surface until smooth, roll out to 5mm thickness. Cut into shapes with 5cm-wide heart-shaped cutter.

Place on lightly greased oven trays, bake in slow oven 25 minutes or until lightly browned. Remove from oven, spread a little Icing on each hot biscuit, sprinkle with toasted almonds.

Icing: Beat egg white lightly with fork or whisk, whisk in icing sugar and flour, tint pale pink with food coloring.

■ **TO FREEZE:** Uniced biscuits will freeze for up to 2 months.

Note: This recipe is not suitable to microwave.

Makes about 20 biscuits.

PECAN TARTLETS

Corn syrup is an imported product. If unavailable, use Maple Flavored Syrup; it is a good locally made substitute available at supermarkets.

PASTRY
¾ cup plain flour
½ cup self-raising flour
2 tablespoons custard powder
2 tablespoons icing sugar
125g butter
1 tablespoon iced water, approximately
FILLING
¾ cup (100g) chopped pecan nuts
¼ cup brown sugar
2 teaspoons plain flour
½ cup corn syrup
2 teaspoons melted butter
1 egg

Pastry: Sift flours, custard powder and icing sugar into bowl, rub in butter. Add enough iced water to bind ingredients together. Knead on lightly floured surface until smooth, cover in plastic food wrap, refrigerate 30 minutes. Roll Pastry between 2 sheets of plastic food wrap; cut into rounds with fluted cutter large enough to line patty pans. Divide pecans between cases, pour Filling into cases. Bake in moderate oven 15 minutes or until golden brown.

Filling: Toast pecans on oven tray in moderate oven for 5 minutes; cool. Combine brown sugar, flour, corn syrup, butter and egg in small bowl, beat with electric mixer until smooth.

Makes about 25.

■ **TO FREEZE:** Baked tartlets will freeze well for up to 2 months.

Note: This recipe is not suitable to microwave.

LEMON CREAM DIAMONDS

This recipe can be made the day before required and stored in an airtight container. Lemon Butter can be made several weeks ahead of time and stored covered in refrigerator.

500g packet buttercake mix
300ml carton thickened cream, whipped
LEMON BUTTER
2 eggs
⅓ cup sugar
2 teaspoons grated lemon rind
¼ cup lemon juice
2 tablespoons water
60g butter, chopped

Make cake mix according to instructions on packet. Pour into greased and lined swiss roll tin (base measures 25cm x 30cm), bake in moderate oven 30 minutes or until golden brown. Turn onto wire rack to cool; refrigerate until cold. Split cake in half horizontally with sharp knife, spread bottom half of cake with Lemon Butter and cream, replace top. Refrigerate covered for at least 30 minutes. Use sharp serrated knife to cut into diamond shapes. Dust tops with sifted icing sugar just before serving. Decorate with sliced strawberries, if desired.

Lemon Butter: Beat eggs and sugar together with fork until well combined. Add lemon rind and juice, water and butter. Place in top of double saucepan or in a bowl over hot water, stir over simmering water for about 10 minutes or until mixture thickens slightly, cool, refrigerate before using.

Makes 20.

■ **TO FREEZE:** Cakes can be made, cooled, left unfilled wrapped in freezer wrap and frozen for up to 2 months.

Note: This recipe is not suitable to microwave.

Back from left: Fudgy Peanut Butter Cake; Pecan Tartlets; Almond Heart Biscuits.
Front from left: Cheese-Topped Scones; Lemon Cream Diamonds.
China is Royal Doulton Sweet Violets.

Brunches are becoming a popular way to entertain friends in a relaxed, casual way. A lot of the recipes can be prepared ahead to save you time on the morning of the brunch.

LEISURELY BRUNCH FOR EIGHT

CHEESE SOUFFLE IN TOMATOES

BRANDIED MUSHROOM PIES

APRICOT MUESLI MUFFINS

FOUR FRUIT CRUMBLE

SALAMI SIZZLERS

WHOLEMEAL SPINACH AND CHEESE LOAF

PAN FRIED POTATOES AND BACON

Buy some extra frozen or fresh croissants and/or Danish pastries to serve, also some fresh fruit, particularly if the weather is warm. Serve a selection of teas, coffee, wine or champagne — all are acceptable; so much depends on your guests and the weather.

CHEESE SOUFFLE IN TOMATOES

Tomatoes can be prepared up to 12 hours before cooking. Filling can also be made, except for the beating and folding in of egg whites; do this as close to cooking time as possible

8 medium tomatoes
30g butter
1 tablespoon plain flour
⅔ cup milk
2 eggs, separated
¾ cup grated tasty cheese
2 tablespoons grated parmesan cheese

Cut top from tomatoes. Scoop out flesh with spoon; reserve flesh for another use. Drain tomatoes upside down on absorbent paper.

Melt butter in pan, add flour, cook stirring 1 minute. Add milk gradually, stir over heat until mixture boils and thickens. Remove from heat, stir in egg yolks, tasty cheese and half the parmesan cheese. Beat egg whites until soft peaks form, gently fold cheese mixture into egg whites. Divide filling between tomatoes, sprinkle top with remaining cheese. Bake in moderate oven 10 minutes. Serve immediately.
Note: This recipe is not suitable to freeze or microwave.

BRANDIED MUSHROOM PIES

Pies can be assembled in dishes the day before cooking, if desired.

45g butter
2 onions, sliced
1kg baby mushrooms, halved
2 tablespoons brandy
1 tablespoon cornflour
2 × 300ml cartons sour cream
2 sheets ready-rolled puff pastry
1 egg, lightly beaten

Heat butter in large pan, add onions, cook stirring until lightly browned, add mushrooms, cook over high heat until just soft. Add brandy, cook until liquid evaporates, add blended cornflour and sour cream, stir until mixture boils and thickens, cool to room temperature.

Divide mixture between 8 souffle dishes (½-cup capacity). Cut each pastry sheet into 4 squares. Cut a 1cm strip from edges of each square. Press this strip of pastry around inside rim of each souffle dish; strips should wrap round dishes twice (see photograph below). Brush pastry around rim with a little water. Place square of pastry on top, press to seal pastry to rim. Trim pastry, decorate edge, brush with egg. Bake in moderately hot oven 20 minutes or until golden brown.
    Makes 8.
Note: This recipe is not suitable to freeze or microwave.

FOUR FRUIT CRUMBLE

Prepare fruit mixture (except banana) and Crumble Topping separately up to several hours before serving. Assemble just before cooking.

825g can plums, drained, pitted
2 × 250g punnets strawberries, halved
2 bananas, sliced
2 passionfruit
½ cup cream
⅓ cup coconut
CRUMBLE TOPPING
½ cup plain flour
½ cup brown sugar
½ cup quick cooking oats
½ teaspoon cinnamon
60g butter

Combine plums, strawberries, bananas, passionfruit pulp, cream and coconut. Place into 8 individual dishes (½-cup capacity), sprinkle with Crumble Topping. Bake in moderate oven 15 minutes or until browned and bubbly; stand for 5 minutes before serving with whipped cream, if desired.
Crumble Topping: Combine flour, sugar, oats and cinnamon in bowl, rub in butter.
Note: This recipe is not suitable to freeze or microwave.

OPPOSITE PAGE
Clockwise from front: Brandied Mushroom Pies; Salami Sizzlers; Apricot Muesli Muffins; Cheese Souffle in Tomatoes; Pan Fried Potatoes and Bacon; Wholemeal Spinach and Cheese Loaf; Four Fruit Crumble.
China is Duche by Studio Haus.

WHOLEMEAL SPINACH AND CHEESE LOAF

This can be made up to an hour before cooking. Dough and Filling can be made up to several hours beforehand.

WHOLEMEAL CRUST
15g compressed yeast
1 teaspoon sugar
¾ cup warm milk
1½ cups plain white flour
1 cup plain wholemeal flour
⅓ cup kibbled rye
1 tablespoon sugar, extra
½ teaspoon salt
1 tablespoon oil
SPINACH FILLING
6 spinach leaves, chopped
1 onion, sliced
1 clove garlic, crushed
1 tablespoon oil
250g mushrooms, sliced
1 small red pepper, chopped
CHEESE FILLING
200g ricotta cheese
⅓ cup grated parmesan cheese
2 egg yolks
1 teaspoon lemon juice
6 black olives, halved

Wholemeal Crust: Cream yeast with sugar, stir in milk, stand covered in warm place for 10 minutes or until foamy. Sift flours into large bowl, add rye, extra sugar and salt. Make well in centre, add yeast mixture and oil, mix to a firm dough. Turn onto lightly floured surface, knead 5 minutes or until smooth and elastic. Put into greased bowl, cover, stand in warm place 30 minutes or until doubled in bulk. Punch dough down, turn onto lightly floured surface, knead until smooth, roll out dough to a rectangle measuring 26cm × 38cm. Lift dough into greased rectangular ovenproof dish (base measures 14cm × 24cm) to cover base and sides; trim edges, reserve scraps of dough. Spread Spinach Filling over dough, then Cheese Filling over spinach. Roll out scraps of dough to a rectangle. Cut into strips about 1.5cm wide, place over Cheese Filling in a lattice pattern. Place olives between lattice strips, brush dough with a little oil. Bake in moderately hot oven 35 minutes or until crust is golden brown; stand 10 minutes before cutting.

Spinach Filling: Heat oil in pan, add onion and garlic, cook few minutes, add spinach and mushrooms, cook stirring until spinach has just wilted. Place in strainer, press with spoon to extract as much liquid as possible; stir in red pepper.

Cheese Filling: Puree ricotta and parmesan cheese, egg yolks and lemon juice with electric mixer, blender or processor until smooth.

Note: This recipe is not suitable to freeze or microwave.

PAN FRIED POTATOES AND BACON

Boil or steam potatoes a day before required, peel and dice on day of cooking. This is a great way to use up leftover boiled potatoes.

750g potatoes
2 tablespoons plain flour
4 green shallots, chopped
½ cup cream
4 bacon rashers, finely chopped

Peel and dice potatoes, boil or steam 5 minutes or until tender; drain, place in bowl, mix in flour, shallots and cream. Cook bacon in large pan until crisp, pour potato mixture over bacon in pan, cook over medium heat until potato mixture browns underneath. Turn mixture over with an egg slide, brown on other side, serve immediately.

Note: This recipe is not suitable to freeze or microwave.

SALAMI SIZZLERS

Topping for bread can be prepared up to 12 hours before serving, except for folding in of egg whites.

100g salami, chopped
1 cup grated tasty cheese
1 tablespoon finely chopped black olives
2 green shallots, chopped
2 eggs, separated
8 slices bread

Combine salami with cheese, olives, shallots and egg yolks. Beat egg whites until soft peaks form, gently fold into salami mixture. Grill bread slices on one side, turn over, spread with salami mixture, grill until browned; serve immediately.

Note: This recipe is not suitable to freeze or microwave.

Above: Wholemeal Spinach and Cheese Loaf.
Right: Salami Sizzlers; Pan Fried Potatoes and Bacon.

APRICOT MUESLI MUFFINS

Muffins can be made a day in advance, wrapped in foil and reheated just before serving.

1 cup (150g) finely chopped dried apricots
2 teaspoons grated orange rind
1 cup orange juice
1 cup buttermilk
125g butter, melted
½ cup honey
2 eggs, lightly beaten
1½ cups wholemeal self-raising flour
1 cup white self-raising flour
1½ cups toasted muesli
½ cup wheatgerm
TOPPING
⅓ cup brown sugar
½ teaspoon cinnamon
30g butter, melted
2 tablespoons plain flour
½ cup toasted muesli

Combine apricots, orange rind and juice in bowl, stand 15 minutes. Stir in buttermilk, butter, honey and eggs. Combine flours, muesli and wheatgerm in bowl, make a well in centre, add apricot mixture, stir lightly until just mixed. Fill greased muffin tins three quarters full of mixture. Sprinkle with Topping, bake in moderately hot oven 20 minutes, or until golden brown.

Topping: Combine all ingredients and mix until crumbly.

■ **TO MICROWAVE:** Cook 6 muffins at a time on HIGH 2½ minutes; stand few minutes before serving.

■ **TO FREEZE:** Cool muffins, wrap, in single layer, seal. Freeze up to 4 weeks. Thaw muffins wrapped in foil in moderate oven about 20 minutes.

Makes 24.

Cocktail parties are gaining popularity again as an easy way to entertain a large number of guests for a fairly short time. The recognised cocktail hour is between 6pm and 8pm.

COCKTAIL PARTY FOR 20

OYSTERS WITH SMOKED SALMON

CREAMY STUFFED EGGS

SPINACH IN MUSHROOM CAPS

SMOKED TROUT PATE

CRUDITES WITH GREEN MAYONNAISE

CHECKERBOARD SANDWICHES

SMOKED OYSTER QUICHE WEDGES

ANCHOVY PIZZA FINGERS

SOUR CREAM CHICKEN SATE

SWEET AND SOUR CHICKEN STICKS

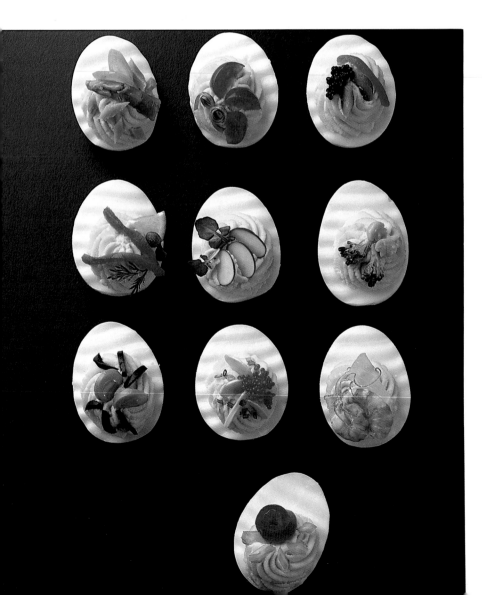

OYSTERS WITH SMOKED SALMON

Assemble up to 6 hours before serving time. Keep covered in refrigerator.

24 oysters in shells
½ cup mayonnaise
1 teaspoon lemon juice
5 slices smoked salmon
1 tablespoon chopped chives
Puree mayonnaise, lemon juice and 4 slices of the smoked salmon in blender or processor until smooth. Spoon mixture over oysters, garnish with strips of remaining smoked salmon. Sprinkle with chives, cover, refrigerate until serving.
   Makes 24.
Note: This recipe is not suitable to freeze.

CREAMY STUFFED EGGS

Prepare eggs up to 6 hours before serving. Keep covered in refrigerator.

12 small eggs
1 tablespoon mayonnaise
1 tablespoon sour cream
1 teaspoon french mustard
Place eggs in large pan, cover with cold water, stir constantly but gently over high heat until water comes to boil. Stop stirring, boil uncovered 10 minutes; drain. Crack shells of eggs, place eggs in bowl covered with cold water, stand 1 hour. Remove shells, cut eggs in half lengthwise. Combine egg yolks, mayonnaise, sour cream and french mustard; mix well until smooth. Pipe mixture into egg whites and decorate as desired. See photograph for ideas.
   Makes 24.
Note: This recipe is not suitable to freeze or microwave.

SPINACH IN MUSHROOM CAPS

Filling can be prepared a day ahead of serving time, store covered in refrigerator. Keep mushroom caps in paper bag in refrigerator. Assemble caps up to several hours before serving.

24 baby mushrooms
2 bacon rashers, finely chopped
1 small onion, finely chopped
60g ricotta cheese
30g feta cheese
½ x 250g packet frozen chopped spinach, thawed

Remove stems from mushrooms, chop stems finely. Cook bacon in pan stirring until crisp, drain on absorbent paper. Drain all but 2 teaspoons of bacon fat from pan, add onion and mushroom stems to bacon fat, cook stirring until onion is soft. Process ricotta and feta cheeses until smooth, add bacon and onion mixture. Press out as much liquid as possible from spinach, add to cheese mixture, process until smooth. Fill mushroom caps with spinach mixture. Garnish with tiny wedges of cherry tomato, if desired.

Makes 24.
Note: This recipe is not suitable to freeze or microwave.

SMOKED TROUT PATE

This pate will keep covered in refrigerator for up to 1 week. Allow pate to come to room temperature before piping or spreading onto toast, pumpernickel rounds or water biscuits.

250g smoked trout
125g packet cream cheese, softened
125g unsalted butter, softened
2 tablespoons lemon juice
dash tabasco sauce
2 teaspoons horseradish cream
2 tablespoons chopped chives

Remove skin and bones from trout. Puree trout in processor until smooth, add cheese, butter, lemon juice, tabasco and horseradish cream, process until smooth. Stir in chives. Decorate with canned pimiento strips and caviar, if desired.

Makes about 1½ cups.
■ **TO FREEZE:** Freeze Pate in airtight container for up to 4 weeks.

CRUDITES WITH GREEN MAYONNAISE

Make mayonnaise up to 2 days ahead of serving, if desired. Stored covered in refrigerator. Choose all or some of the vegetables suggested below to serve with the Mayonnaise.

1 bunch baby radishes
3 celery sticks
125g green beans
60g snow peas
250g punnet cherry tomatoes
125g baby mushrooms
2 small carrots
GREEN MAYONNAISE
1 cup mayonnaise
1 tablespoon chopped parsley
1 tablespoon chopped watercress
1 tablespoon chopped chives
2 teaspoons french mustard

Cut celery into small sticks, peel and cut carrots into sticks. Top and tail beans, cut into 8cm lengths, top and tail snow peas, add beans to pan of boiling water, boil 1 minute, add snow peas, boil further 1 minute, drain, rinse under cold water, drain. Arrange radishes, celery, tomatoes, mushrooms, carrots, beans and snow peas around a bowl of Green Mayonnaise.

Green Mayonnaise: Blend mayonnaise with herbs and mustard, mix well.

Makes about 1¼ cups.
Note: This recipe is not suitable to freeze.

ABOVE
Left to right: on square platter, Spinach in Mushroom Caps; Oysters with Smoked Salmon; Smoked Trout Pate; in oval dish, Crudites with Green Mayonnaise.
LEFT
Creamy Stuffed Eggs.
China is Villeroy and Boch Vieux Luxembourg.

SMOKED OYSTER QUICHE WEDGES

Quiche can be made a day ahead of serving and reheated in moderate oven uncovered for about 5 minutes.

PARMESAN PASTRY
1½ cups plain flour
¼ cup grated parmesan cheese
125g butter
1 tablespoon water, approximately
1 tablespoon parmesan cheese, extra
FILLING
300ml carton thickened cream
2 eggs, lightly beaten
105g can smoked oysters, drained
1 teaspoon french mustard
1 tablespoon mayonnaise
1 small red pepper, finely chopped
6 green shallots, finely chopped
1 tablespoon chopped stuffed olives

Parmesan Pastry: Process combined flour, cheese and butter until fine. With motor running, add enough water to make ingredients cling together. Wrap dough in plastic food wrap, refrigerate 30 minutes. Roll pastry between 2 pieces of plastic food wrap. Line 6 flan tins with removable bases (base measures 11cm) with pastry. Pierce with fork, sprinkle with extra cheese. Bake in moderately hot oven 7 minutes. Remove from oven, spoon in Filling, reduce heat to moderate, bake 10 minutes or until Filling is set. Stand few minutes before cutting into quarters. Garnish with extra sliced olives.

Filling: Combine cream, eggs, chopped oysters, mustard, mayonnaise, pepper, shallots and olives.

■ **TO FREEZE:** Bake pastry cases as above, cool. Spoon in Filling, place on oven trays in freezer. Freeze until firm, then wrap in freezer wrap, freeze up to 2 months. To serve, bake on trays, uncovered, while frozen 30 minutes in moderate oven or, until Filling is set.

Makes 24.

Note: This recipe is not suitable to microwave.

CHECKERBOARD SANDWICHES

Slice and refrigerate covered up to 2 hours before serving. Use half or the whole loaf, if desired.

1 large loaf unsliced white bread
SMOKED SALMON FILLING
350g smoked salmon, chopped
180g butter, softened
2 tablespoons lemon juice
1 teaspoon french mustard
4 green shallots, chopped
HERB CREAM CHEESE FILLING
500g packaged cream cheese, softened
¼ cup chopped chives
¼ cup chopped parsley
4 green shallots, chopped
2 tablespoons cream
1 teaspoon french mustard

STEP 1
Remove crusts from bread. Cut in half crosswise.

STEP 2
Cut lengthwise into 1cm slices using serrated knife. Sandwich slices together with Smoked Salmon Filling. Wrap in plastic food wrap, refrigerate 30 minutes or until firm.

STEP 3

Slice loaf crosswise into 1cm slices.

STEP 4

Sandwich these slices together with Herb Cream Cheese Filling, as shown. Wrap in plastic food wrap, refrigerate 30 minutes or until firm.

STEP 5:

Slice loaf as shown to show pattern. Cut each slice in half crosswise; then cut each in half diagonally. Repeat with remaining half loaf of bread.

Smoked Salmon Filling: Combine all ingredients in processor, process until smooth.

Herb Cream Cheese Filling: Combine all ingredients in processor, process until smooth.

Makes about 60.

■ **TO FREEZE:** Freeze layered loaf for up to 4 weeks. Thaw for about 2 hours before slicing.

Left: Smoked Oyster Quiche Wedges.
Right: Anchovy Pizza Fingers;
Checkerboard Sandwiches.

ANCHOVY PIZZA FINGERS

Pizzas can be baked up to 12 hours before serving. Reheat uncovered in moderate oven for 5 minutes.

DOUGH
2 cups plain flour
¾ cup warm water
7g sachet dried yeast
1 teaspoon sugar
TOPPING
¼ cup tomato paste
30g butter
1 onion, finely chopped
1 clove garlic, crushed
6 black olives, pitted, chopped
1 teaspoon ground rosemary
45g can anchovy fillets, drained, rinsed, chopped
1 small red pepper, finely chopped
¼ cup grated parmesan cheese
2 cups (200g) grated mozzarella cheese

Dough: Sift flour into large bowl, stir in combined water, yeast and sugar, mix to a firm dough, knead on lightly floured surface until smooth. Divide dough in half, roll each half out large enough to cover base of 2 × 28cm pizza pans. Spread each with tomato paste. Heat butter in pan, add onion, cook stirring until lightly browned, stir in garlic, remove from heat, stir in olives, rosemary, anchovies and pepper. Sprinkle pizzas with combined cheeses, then anchovy mixture. Bake in hot oven for 20 minutes or until well browned. Cut into finger lengths to serve.

Makes about 50.

■ **TO FREEZE:** Freeze uncooked pizza for up to 4 weeks. Bake uncovered in hot oven for about 25 minutes.

Note: This recipe is not suitable to microwave.

SOUR CREAM CHICKEN SATE

Chicken can be marinated in the sauce, covered in the refrigerator, for up to 2 days ahead of cooking time. Soak bamboo skewers overnight in cold water to prevent burning.

6 large (about 1kg) chicken breast fillets
2 tablespoons peanut butter
1 cup sour cream
1 tablespoon lemon juice
2 teaspoons grated fresh ginger
2 teaspoons ground coriander
4 green shallots, chopped

Cut chicken into 2cm cubes, add to combined peanut butter, sour cream, lemon juice, ginger, coriander and shallots. Cover, refrigerate overnight or for at least 2 hours. Thread 3 chicken pieces onto each skewer. Grill gently until cooked through and lightly browned; do not turn.

Makes about 25.

Note: This recipe is not suitable to freeze or microwave.

Above, Sweet and Sour Chicken Sticks; below, Sour Cream Chicken Sate.

SWEET AND SOUR CHICKEN STICKS

Chicken can be marinated up to 2 days before required.

20 large chicken wings
⅔ cup canned pineapple juice
2 tablespoons white vinegar
¼ cup tomato sauce
1 teaspoon soy sauce
2 tablespoons sugar
1 onion, grated
1 clove garlic, crushed
1 tablespoon cornflour
¼ cup water

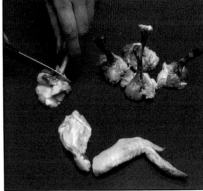

Using a sharp knife, cut off the thicker, meatier section of the wing at the first joint. This is the only section used in the recipe. Remaining parts of the wing can be cooked or frozen for another use.

Holding end of bone and using sharp knife, trim around bone to cut meat free. Scrape and push meat down to large end (see photograph above). Pull skin and meat down over end of bone.

Combine pineapple juice, vinegar, sauces, sugar, onion and garlic. Pour over chicken, marinate at least 2 hours. Remove chicken from marinade, place upright into baking dish, bake in moderate oven 30 minutes or until tender and browned. Remove chicken to serving dish, pour any remaining marinade into baking dish, heat on top of stove. Blend cornflour with water, add to marinade, stir until mixture boils and thickens; strain. If mixture is too thick, add a little more pineapple juice. Pour over chicken to serve.

Makes 20.

■ **TO MICROWAVE:** Prepare and marinate chicken, as above. Cook chicken in shallow dish in about 2 lots; cook on HIGH 10 minutes or until tender. Brush occasionally with marinade. Remove chicken to serving dish, pour remaining marinade into dish, stir in blended cornflour and water, cook on HIGH 3 minutes or until mixture boils and thickens, stir once.

■ **TO FREEZE:** Chicken sticks can be frozen for up to 2 months. Thaw and marinate when required. Marinade is not suitable to freeze.

DELICIOUS DETAILS

TO SEGMENT ORANGES

Choose large firm ripe oranges, peel thickly with sharp knife, removing as much white pith as possible. Work over bowl to catch juice from oranges. Cut down between membranes joining orange segments. Be careful not to cut right through, just to the centre of the orange is all that's needed; remove any seeds as you work.

TO MAKE TOMATO ROSES
STEP 1

Choose well-shaped, firm red tomatoes of small to medium size. Start from bottom end (not stem end) of tomato, peel thinly with a small sharp knife in a circular action. Be careful not to break tomato peel.

STEP 2

Starting from where peeling began, twist tomato peel into rose shape, as shown. If a large rose is required, it is easier to twist peel into rose shape around fingertip.

The recipes we have chosen for you are deliciously different. They all have a Mediterranean flavor, and will impress family or friends at your next barbecue.

MEDITERRANEAN STYLE BARBECUE FOR 10

TASTY MINCE 'N' MINT KEBABS

LAMB IN GARLIC MARINADE

SCHNAPPER CUTLET PARCELS

CHICK PEA AND SPINACH SALAD

FENNEL SALAD

PEPPER, FETA AND OLIVE SALAD

LEMON PEPPER BREAD

ORANGE APRICOT YOGHURT ICECREAM

WALNUT AND HONEY STRUDEL PARCELS

TASTY MINCE 'N' MINT KEBABS

Kebabs can be prepared a day ahead of barbecue; cover, refrigerate until time to barbecue. You will need to boil a tablespoon or two of rice for this recipe. Soak wooden skewers overnight in cold water to prevent burning.

250g sausage mince
250g minced steak
1 onion, grated
2 cloves garlic, crushed
1 teaspoon grated lemon rind
1 teaspoon lemon juice
1 teaspoon mixed herbs
¼ cup chopped parsley
¼ cup cooked rice
1 tablespoon tomato paste
1 egg, lightly beaten
MINT DIP
¼ cup mint jelly
1 tablespoon french dressing
2 teaspoons chopped mint (or ½ teaspoon dried mint leaves)

Left: Tasty Mince 'n' Mint Kebabs. Above, left to right: Pepper, Feta and Olive Salad; Lemon Pepper Bread; Lamb in Garlic Marinade; Schnapper Cutlet Parcels; Fennel Salad; Chick Pea and Spinach Salad.

Combine all ingredients, mix well. Shape tablespoonfuls of mixture into flat rolls around the end of 20 soaked wooden skewers, cover, refrigerate 30 minutes. Barbecue until kebabs are browned all over and cooked through. Serve with Mint Dip.

Mint Dip: Combine mint jelly and dressing in pan, stir over low heat until jelly is melted, stir in mint.

■ **TO MICROWAVE:** Place kebabs on a flat dish, cook on HIGH 2 minutes, turn kebabs, cook on HIGH 1 minute or until tender.

Mint Dip: Combine mint jelly and dressing, cook on HIGH 1 minute or until jelly is melted, stir in mint.

■ **TO FREEZE:** Shape kebabs onto skewers, place in single layer on oven tray covered with plastic food wrap. Cover, freeze until firm, remove from tray, wrap in foil, freeze up for to 4 weeks. Mint Dip is not suitable to freeze.

Barbecue is from Barbecues Galore; China is Claude by Studio Haus.

LAMB IN GARLIC MARINADE

Marinate lamb overnight for best flavor. Cooking time depends on heat of barbecue and personal preference.

2 x 1½ kg boned out shoulders (or forequarters) of lamb
2 large cloves garlic, peeled
MARINADE
2 onions, finely sliced
3 teaspoons grated lemon rind
⅓ cup lemon juice
1½ teaspoons dried basil leaves
1½ teaspoons dried oregano leaves
¼ cup olive oil
1½ cups dry white wine

Lay lamb flat on bench, trim off any excess fat. Cut garlic into thin slivers, push into meat in several places. Place lamb in large bowl, add Marinade, cover, refrigerate overnight.

Next day, pat lamb dry, place on rack over low-heat part of barbecue. Brush with Marinade, cook turning and brushing with Marinade for about 50 minutes or until cooked as desired.

Marinade: Combine all ingredients, mix well.

Note: This recipe is not suitable to freeze or microwave.

SCHNAPPER CUTLET PARCELS

Rice topping can be made a day before required, if desired. Assemble parcels up to 12 hours before the barbecue. We boiled ⅓ cup rice for this recipe.

10 schnapper cutlets
1 cup cooked rice
2 green shallots, chopped
1 teaspoon grated lemon rind
¼ teaspoon ground cumin
2 large tomatoes, thinly sliced

Combine rice, shallots, lemon rind and cumin, press onto one side of each fish cutlet, top each with a slice of tomato. Wrap each in a square of greased foil, fold foil over at top. Barbecue gently for 20 minutes or until fish is tender.

Note: This recipe is not suitable to freeze or microwave.

CHICK PEA AND SPINACH SALAD

Chick peas can be prepared up to 2 days before required, if desired.

1½ cups dry chick peas
½ bunch English spinach leaves, shredded
1 small radicchio lettuce
1 small mignonette lettuce
HOT DRESSING
3 tablespoons olive oil
2 cloves garlic, crushed
1 small onion, finely chopped
2 tablespoons white vinegar
1 tablespoon lemon juice
1 teaspoon sugar
1 teaspoon grainy mustard
½ teaspoon dried marjoram leaves
2 tablespoons chopped mint

Soak chick peas in water overnight. Next day, drain, rinse, place in pan, cover with water, cover, boil 10 minutes. Reduce heat, simmer covered 50 minutes, drain, rinse under cold water, cool. Combine chick peas with spinach, serve on lettuce leaves, top with Hot Dressing just before serving.
Hot Dressing: Heat oil in pan, add onion and garlic, cook stirring until onion is soft. Add vinegar, lemon juice, sugar, mustard, marjoram and mint.
Note: This recipe is not suitable to freeze or microwave.

FENNEL SALAD

Assemble salad ingredients up to 12 hours before serving, if desired. Make Dressing a day before, if desired.

2 fennel bulbs, thinly sliced
2 tomatoes
1 cucumber, peeled
1 cos lettuce
3 green shallots, chopped
DRESSING
⅓ cup olive oil
⅓ cup lemon juice
1 clove garlic, crushed
¼ teaspoon dried oregano leaves
2 tablespoons chopped basil (or 1 teaspoon dried basil leaves)

Cut tomatoes into wedges, cut cucumber into strips; tear lettuce into pieces. Combine all salad ingredients in bowl, pour Dressing over, toss well.
Dressing: Combine all ingredients in screwtop jar, shake well.
Note: This recipe is not suitable to freeze.

PEPPER, FETA AND OLIVE SALAD

Prepare salad up to a day before required, if desired; add dressing just before serving.

2 red peppers, chopped
2 green peppers, chopped
1 onion, chopped
500g baby mushrooms, sliced
250g feta cheese, cubed
18 (60g) pitted black olives
3 tablespoons chopped parsley
½ cup bottled italian dressing

Combine peppers, onions and mushrooms in bowl. Add cheese, olives and parsley. Before serving toss lightly in dressing.
Note: This recipe is not suitable to freeze.

LEMON PEPPER BREAD

6 rounds flat lebanese bread
125g butter
2 cloves garlic, crushed
½ teaspoon lemon pepper
1 teaspoon grated lemon rind
2 tablespoons parmesan cheese

Split bread in half horizontally. Melt butter in pan, add garlic, lemon pepper, lemon rind and cheese. Brush mixture lightly over cut side of bread. Barbecue on hot plate for about 5 minutes, turn often.
■ **TO MICROWAVE:** Combine butter, garlic, lemon pepper, lemon rind and parmesan cheese in bowl, cook on HIGH 1 minute.
■ **TO FREEZE:** Freeze flavored butter for up to 4 weeks.

ORANGE APRICOT YOGHURT ICECREAM

Icecream can be made 2 weeks ahead. Sauce can be made up to several days ahead, if desired.

125g dried apricots
300ml carton thickened cream
1 teaspoon grated orange rind
200g carton natural yoghurt
3 egg yolks
¾ cup sugar
2 tablespoons orange curacao
½ cup orange juice
1 tablespoon lemon juice
ORANGE LIQUEUR SAUCE
6 oranges
2 tablespoons orange curacao
1 cup sugar
1 cup water
2 tablespoons lemon juice

Left: Orange Apricot Yoghurt Icecream. Opposite page: Walnut and Honey Strudel Parcels.

Soak apricots covered in cold water 1 hour. Place apricots and water in pan, bring to boil, reduce heat, simmer 15 minutes or until apricots are tender; drain. Puree apricots in blender or processor. Heat cream, orange rind and yoghurt in pan. Beat egg yolks and sugar in small bowl with electric mixer until thick, gradually beat in hot mixture. Return mixture to pan, whisk over heat without boiling until slightly thickened. Stir in apricot puree, liqueur, orange juice and lemon juice. Pour mixture into loaf tin, cover with foil, freeze until partly frozen. Beat with electric mixer until smooth, return to loaf tin, cover, freeze overnight. Serve with Orange Liqueur Sauce.

Orange Liqueur Sauce: Peel oranges thickly, cut into segments over bowl, (see page 117) squeeze excess juice (you will need ½ cup juice) from orange membranes, stir in liqueur. Combine sugar and water in pan, stir over heat without boiling until sugar is dissolved. Bring to boil, boil rapidly 5 minutes; cool. Stir in lemon juice. Pour Sauce over oranges, cover refrigerate.

■ **TO FREEZE:** Freeze icecream covered for up to 2 weeks.

WALNUT AND HONEY STRUDEL PARCELS

Filling can be made the day before required, if desired. Parcels can be assembled up to 2 hours ahead of cooking time, cover, refrigerate.

250g packet cream cheese
2 tablespoons honey
¼ cup castor sugar
2 teaspoons grated lemon rind
2 cups (200g) chopped walnuts
125g unsalted butter
10 sheets fillo pastry

Beat cream cheese, honey and sugar until smooth, stir in lemon rind and walnuts, refrigerate. Brush one sheet of pastry with melted butter, place another sheet on top, continue with butter and pastry to use 5 sheets. Repeat with remaining butter and pastry. Place half the cream cheese mixture on corner of each rectangle of pastry, roll up diagonally like a parcel, as shown left, tucking in edges. Brush parcels with butter, make diagonal cuts across top of each one. Place onto oven tray, bake in moderately hot oven 30 minutes or until golden brown. Serve sliced with whipped cream.

■ **TO FREEZE:** Parcel can be frozen uncooked, covered, for up to a month. Thaw at room temperature 12 hours before cooking.

Note: This recipe is not suitable to microwave.

We've chosen a balance of alcoholic and non-alcoholic drinks for you from sparkling punches to super special coffees. The size of glasses you use will determine how many guests you can serve from these recipes. We've given quantities in litres (one litre = four metric measuring cups) as a guide.

COCKTAILS, COFFEE AND PUNCHES

SPICY APPLE PUNCH

Apple mixture can be cooked and refrigerated up to 2 days ahead.

3 Granny Smith apples, peeled, cored, sliced
1 cup water
2 tablespoons brown sugar
1 teaspoon grated fresh ginger
2 × 750ml bottles sparkling alcoholic apple cider
750ml bottle lemonade
1 Granny Smith apple, peeled, cored, sliced, extra

Combine apples, water, sugar and ginger in pan, bring to boil, cover, reduce heat, simmer 10 minutes or until apple is pulpy. Remove from heat, puree in blender or processor until smooth, cool, refrigerate until cold. When ready to serve, add apple cider and lemonade to apple mixture, serve with extra apple.

Makes about 3 litres.

ORANGE AND APRICOT PUNCH

2 cups orange juice
2 tablespoons lemon juice
425ml can apricot nectar
1 apple, quartered, sliced
2 × 285ml bottles tonic water

Combine juices and apricot nectar in bowl, add apple. Refrigerate for 1 hour. When ready to serve, stir in well chilled tonic water.

Makes about 1½ litres.

RHUBARB AND STRAWBERRY PUNCH

500g frozen rhubarb
¼ cup icing sugar
250g punnet strawberries
1½ tablespoons lemon juice
½ teaspoon grated fresh ginger
375ml can lemonade

Puree thawed rhubarb and icing sugar in blender or processor, strain, discard pulp. Puree strawberries and lemon juice, add to rhubarb juice. Stir in ginger and lemonade just before serving. Serve with extra strawberries, if desired.

Makes about 1 litre.

DRY GINGER AND LEMON PUNCH

750ml bottle Claytons
½ cup lemon juice
1 teaspoon Angostura Bitters
1.25 litre bottle dry ginger ale
750ml bottle lemonade
1 lemon, sliced

Combine Claytons, lemon juice and Bitters. When ready to serve, add ginger ale and lemonade. Serve with lemon slices.

Makes about 3 litres.

BELOW
From left: Iced Cinnamon Coffee; Special Dessert Coffee.
OPPOSITE PAGE
Clockwise from front: Orange and Apricot Punch; Spicy Apple Punch; Dry Ginger and Lemon Punch; Rhubarb and Strawberry Punch.
Punch glasses are Spin by Kosta-Boda.

SPECIAL DESSERT COFFEES

Substitute your favorite liqueurs in this recipe to create your own Special Coffees. Frost the edge of the glasses by dipping in lemon juice, then in castor sugar. Make sure you prepare extra coffee; your guests are sure to want refills. There is enough Topping for about 10 coffees.

1½ tablespoons Grand Marnier
1½ tablespoons Creme de Cacao
1 cup hot coffee, approximately
TOPPING
300ml carton thickened cream
2 tablespoons Grand Marnier, extra

For each serving, place liqueurs in heat-resistant glass or cup, fill three quarters full with coffee, top with a generous spoonful of Topping. Decorate with orange strips, if desired.
Topping: Whip cream and Grand Marnier until soft peaks form.

ICED CINNAMON COFFEE

Coffee mixture can be made up to several days before required; keep refrigerated.

2 tablespoons instant coffee powder
2 tablespoons sugar
⅓ cup hot water
⅓ cup Kahlua or Tia Maria
6 cups (1½ litres) cold milk
vanilla icecream
8 cinnamon sticks
cinnamon

Combine coffee, sugar and water in blender, blend until coffee and sugar are dissolved. Add Kahlua and milk, blend until smooth. Refrigerate coffee mixture, pour into glasses, top with icecream, place a cinnamon stick in each one, sprinkle with cinnamon.

Makes about 2 litres.

CREAMY BANANA COLADA

This rich creamy cocktail is substantial enough to have for lunch by the pool or beach. Make sure coconut milk and pineapple juice are icy cold.

340ml can coconut milk
1½ cups canned pineapple juice
2 ripe bananas, chopped
½ cup white rum

Blend or process coconut milk, pineapple juice, bananas and rum until smooth and creamy. Pour into glasses, decorate with pineapple and toasted coconut, if desired.

Makes about 1 litre.

CASSIS CHAMPAGNE COCKTAIL

Cassis is a blackcurrant-flavored liqueur, Framboise a raspberry-flavored liqueur.

Cassis or Framboise liqueur
750ml bottle champagne
8 sugar cubes

Place one sugar cube in each of 8 glasses, add a capful or 2 teaspoons of liqueur to each glass. Fill each glass with well chilled champagne, serve immediately.

Serves 6 to 8.

Back: Cassis Champagne Cocktail.
Front: Creamy Banana Colada.
Cocktail glasses are Zwiesel Glas.

124

Glossary

Some names, terms and alternatives are included here to help everyone understand and use our recipes perfectly.

ALMONDS:
Flaked: sliced almonds.
Ground: we used packaged commercially ground nuts in our recipes unless otherwise specified.
AMARETTO: an almond-flavoured liqueur.
ARROWROOT: used mostly for thickening. Cornflour can be used as a substitute.
BACON RASHERS: bacon slices.
BAKING POWDER: is a raising agent consisting of an alkali and an acid. It is mostly made from cream of tartar and bicarbonate of soda in the proportions of 1 level teaspoon of cream of tartar to ½ level teaspoon bicarbonate of soda. This is equivalent to 2 teaspoons baking powder.
BENEDICTINE: brandy-based liqueur, flavoured with honey and herbs.
BICARBONATE OF SODA: also known as baking soda.
BREADCRUMBS:
Stale: use 1 or 2 day old white bread made into crumbs by grating, blending or processing.
Packaged Dry: use fine packaged breadcrumbs.
BUTTER: use salted or unsalted (sweet) butter; 125g is equal to 1 stick butter.
BUTTERMILK: is now made by adding a culture to skim milk to give a slightly acid flavour; skim milk can be substituted, if preferred.
CASSIS: is a brandy-based liqueur with a blackcurrant flavour and colour.
CHESTNUT SPREAD; SWEETENED: an imported product available from gourmet delicatessens and some supermarkets; it is sweetened, flavoured pureed chestnuts.
CHICK PEAS: also known as garbanzos, when canned. Cover dried peas well with water, stand overnight. Next day, drain, then boil in plenty of water for about 1 hour or until tender.
CHILLIES: (dried) are available in many different types and sizes. The small ones (bird's eye or bird peppers) are the hottest. Use tight rubber gloves when chopping fresh chillies as they can burn your skin. The seeds are the hottest part of the chillies so remove them to reduce the heat content of recipes.
CHILLI POWDER: the Asian variety is the hottest and is made from ground chillies; it can be used as a substitute for fresh chillies in the proportion of ½ teaspoon ground chilli powder to 1 medium chopped chilli.
CHILLI SAUCE: we used the hot Chinese variety. It consists of chillies, salt and vinegar. We use it sparingly so that you can easily increase amounts in recipes to suit your taste.
COCONUT: use desiccated coconut unless otherwise specified.
To toast: stir coconut in pan over heat until lightly browned.
Cream: available in cans and cartons in supermarkets and Asian stores; coconut milk can be substituted, although it is not as thick.
Milk: can be bought but is also easy to make using desiccated coconut. (Coconut milk is not the liquid inside the mature coconut.) Place 2 cups desiccated coconut in large bowl, cover with 2½ cups hot water, cover, stand until mixture is just warm. Mix with the hand, then strain through a fine sieve or cloth, squeezing out as much liquid as you can. This will give you about 1½ cups thick milk; it can be used when canned coconut cream is specified. The same coconut can be used again; simply add another 2½ cups hot water, and continue as above; this will give you a watery milk. It can be combined with the first, thicker milk and is a good substitute for the canned coconut milk specified in our recipes. It

can be blended or processed for about 2 seconds, then strained as directed.
COINTREAU: is an orange-flavoured liqueur.
COLOURINGS: we used concentrated liquid vegetable food colourings and powder colourings.
CORNFLOUR: cornstarch.
CORN SYRUP: an imported product available from supermarkets, delicatessens and health food stores. It is available in light or dark colour – either can be substituted for the other.
CREAM: is simply a light pouring cream, also known as half 'n' half.
Thickened (whipping): is specified when necessary in recipes.
Sour: a thick commercially cultured soured cream.
CREAM CHEESE: also known as Philly.
CREME DE CACAO: a chocolate-flavoured liqueur.
CURACAO: an orange-flavoured liqueur.
CURRY POWDER: a convenient combination of spices in powdered form. Curry powder consists of chilli, coriander, cumin, fennel, fenugreek and turmeric in varying proportions.
CUSTARD POWDER: pudding mix.
ESSENCE: an extract from fruit and flowers, used as a flavouring.
EVAPORATED MILK: unsweetened canned milk from which water has been extracted by evaporation.
FIVE SPICE POWDER: a pungent mixture of ground spices which include cinnamon, cloves, fennel, star anise and Szechwan peppers.
FLOUR:
White Plain: all-purpose flour.
White Self-Raising: substitute plain (all-purpose) flour and baking powder in the proportion of ¾ metric cup plain flour to 2 level metric teaspoons of baking powder. Sift together several times before using. If using 8oz measuring cup, use 1 cup plain flour to 2 level teaspoons baking powder.
Wholemeal: wholewheat flour without the addition of baking powder.
Wholemeal Self-Raising: (wholewheat) substitute plain wholemeal flour and baking powder in the proportion of ¾ metric cup plain wholemeal flour to 2 level metric teaspoons baking powder; sift together several times before using. If using an 8oz measuring cup use 1 cup plain wholemeal flour to 2 level teaspoons baking powder.
FRAMBOISE: is a raspberry-flavoured liqueur. Creme de Framboises is sweeter.
FRESH HERBS: we have specified when to use fresh or dried herbs. We used dried (not ground) herbs in the proportion of 1:4 for fresh herbs, eg, 1 teaspoon dried herbs instead of 4 teaspoons (1 tablespoon) chopped fresh herbs.
FRUIT MINCE: also known as mincemeat.
GHERKIN: cornichon.
GINGER:
Fresh, Green or Root Ginger: scrape away outside skin and grate, chop or slice ginger as required. Fresh, peeled ginger can be preserved with enough dry sherry to cover; keep in jar in refrigerator; it will keep for months.
Glace: fresh ginger root preserved in sugar syrup; crystallised ginger can be substituted; rinse off the sugar with warm water, dry ginger well before using.
GLUCOSE SYRUP (liquid glucose): is clear with a consistency like honey; it is made from wheat starch; available at health food stores and supermarkets. Do not confuse it with a glucose drink.
GOLDEN SYRUP: maple, pancake syrup or honey can usually be substituted.
GRAINY MUSTARD: a French-style of mustard containing a variety of crushed mustard seeds.
GRAND MARNIER: is an orange-flavoured liqueur.
GRILL, GRILLER: broil, broiler.
GROUND RICE: rice flour can be substituted.
HOISIN SAUCE: is a thick sweet Chinese barbecue sauce made from a mixture of salted black beans, onion and garlic.
HUNDREDS AND THOUSANDS: nonpareils.
JAM: conserve.
KAHLUA: a coffee-flavoured liqueur.

KIRSCH: a cherry-flavoured liqueur.
LAMINGTON TIN: a rectangular slab pan with a depth of 4cm.
LEMON BUTTER: lemon curd or lemon cheese.
MINCED STEAK: ground beef.
MIXED PEEL: a mixture of crystallised citrus peel; also known as candied peel.
OIL: use a light polyunsaturated salad oil.
PEPPERS: capsicum or bell peppers.
PLUM SAUCE: a dipping sauce which consists of plums preserved in vinegar, sweetened with sugar and flavoured with chillies and spices.
PRAWNS: also known as shrimp. Most of the recipes in this book use fresh, uncooked (green) prawns; peel and devein before use.
PUNNET: small basket usually holding about 250g fruit.
RIND: zest.
RUM: we used an underproof dark rum.
White: we use Bacardi rum which is colourless.
SESAME OIL: made from roasted, crushed white sesame seeds. It is always used in small quantities. Do not use for frying.
SHALLOTS: green shallots are known as spring onions in some Australian states; and as scallions in some other countries.
SNOW PEAS: also known as mange tout, sugar peas or Chinese peas.
SOY SAUCE: made from fermented soy beans. The light sauce is generally used with white meat for flavour, and the darker variety with red meat for colour. There is a multi-purpose salt-reduced sauce available, also Japanese soy sauce. It is personal taste which sauce you use.
SPINACH:
English: a soft-leaved vegetable, more delicate in taste than silverbeet ; however, young silverbeet can be substituted for English spinach.
Silverbeet: a large-leafed vegetable; remove white stalk before cooking.
STOCK CUBES: available in beef, chicken or vegetable flavours. If preferred, powdered stock can be used; 1 level teaspoon powdered stock is equivalent to 1 small stock cube.
SUGAR:
We used coarse granulated table sugar, also known as crystal sugar, unless otherwise specified.
Brown: a soft fine-granulated sugar with molasses present which gives it its characteristic colour.
Castor: fine granulated table sugar.
Icing: also known as confectioners' sugar or powdered sugar. We used icing sugar mixture, not pure icing sugar; unless specified.
SULTANAS: seedless white raisins.
SWEETENED CONDENSED MILK: we used canned milk from which 60% of the water had been removed; the remaining milk is then sweetened with sugar.
SWEET POTATO: kumara; an orange-coloured root vegetable.
TABASCO SAUCE: made with vinegar, hot red peppers and salt. Use sparingly.
TASTY CHEESE: use a firm good-tasting cheddar.
TOMATO:
Paste: a concentrated tomato puree used in flavouring soups, stews, sauces.
Sauce: tomato ketchup.
VANILLA ESSENCE: we used imitation vanilla extract.
WILD RICE: from North America but is not a member of the rice family, it is fairly expensive as it is difficult to cultivate but has a distinctive delicious nutty flavour.
WINE: we used good quality red and white wines.
WONTON WRAPPERS: are thin squares or rounds of fresh noodle dough. They are sold frozen; cover with damp cloth to prevent drying while using.
YEAST: 7g dry yeast (2 level metric teaspoons) is equal to 15g fresh compressed yeast.
ZUCCHINI: courgette.

INDEX

QUICK CONVERSION GUIDE

Wherever you live in the world you can use our recipes with the help of our easy-to-follow conversions for all your cooking needs. These conversions are approximate only. The difference between the exact and approximate conversions of liquid and dry measures amounts to only a teaspoon or two, and will not make any difference to your cooking results.

MEASURING EQUIPMENT

The difference between measuring cups internationally is minimal within 2 or 3 teaspoons' difference. (For the record, 1 Australian metric measuring cup will hold approximately 250ml.) The most accurate way of measuring dry ingredients is to weigh them. When measuring liquids use a clear glass or plastic jug with metric markings.

In this book we use metric measuring cups and spoons approved by Standards Australia.

● a graduated set of four cups for measuring dry ingredients; the sizes are marked on the cups.
● a graduated set of four spoons for measuring dry and liquid ingredients; the amounts are marked on the spoons.
● 1 TEASPOON: 5ml.
● 1 TABLESPOON: 20ml.

NOTE: NZ, CANADA, USA AND UK ALL USE 15ml TABLESPOONS.
ALL CUP AND SPOON MEASUREMENTS ARE LEVEL.

DRY MEASURES

METRIC	IMPERIAL
15g	½oz
30g	1oz
60g	2oz
90g	3oz
125g	4oz (¼lb)
155g	5oz
185g	6oz
220g	7oz
250g	8oz (½lb)
280g	9oz
315g	10oz
345g	11oz
375g	12oz (¾lb)
410g	13oz
440g	14oz
470g	15oz
500g	16oz (1lb)
750g	24oz (1½lb)
1kg	32oz (2lb)

LIQUID MEASURES

METRIC	IMPERIAL
30ml	1 fluid oz
60ml	2 fluid oz
100ml	3 fluid oz
125ml	4 fluid oz
150ml	5 fluid oz (¼ pint/1 gill)
190ml	6 fluid oz
250ml	8 fluid oz
300ml	10 fluid oz (½ pint)
500ml	16 fluid oz
600ml	20 fluid oz (1 pint)
1000ml (1 litre)	1¾ pints

WE USE LARGE EGGS WITH AN AVERAGE WEIGHT OF 60g

HELPFUL MEASURES

METRIC	IMPERIAL
3mm	⅛in
6mm	¼in
1cm	½in
2cm	¾in
2.5cm	1in
5cm	2in
6cm	2½in
8cm	3in
10cm	4in
13cm	5in
15cm	6in
18cm	7in
20cm	8in
23cm	9in
25cm	10in
28cm	11in
30cm	12in (1ft)

HOW TO MEASURE

When using the graduated metric measuring cups, it is important to shake the dry ingredients loosely into the required cup. Do not tap the cup on the bench, or pack the ingredients into the cup unless otherwise directed. Level top of cup with knife. When using graduated metric measuring spoons, level top of spoon with knife. When measuring liquids in the jug, place jug on flat surface, check for accuracy at eye level.

OVEN TEMPERATURES

These oven temperatures are only a guide; we've given you the lower degree of heat. Always check the manufacturer's manual.

	C° (Celsius)	F° (Fahrenheit)	Gas Mark
Very slow	120	250	1
Slow	150	300	2
Moderately slow	160	325	3
Moderate	180	350	4
Moderately hot	190	375	5
Hot	200	400	6
Very hot	230	450	7